Ca...

wo... ...gs. She is the owner of Pure Dog Listeners Ltd
and offers seminars and dog-owner consultations, teaching canine
communication methods to correct undesirable behaviour in dogs.
She is also joint inventor of the Happy At Heel harness for all dog
walking problems.

Find out more at www.puredoglisteners.com

Other titles from How To Books

Canine Cuisine
Elaine Everest

Showing Your Dog
Elaine Everest

A New Puppy in the Family
Elaine Everest

The New Puppy Owner's Manual
Angela Fitch

Why Does My Dog Do That?

Caroline Spencer

howtobooks

Constable & Robinson Ltd
55-56 Russell Square
London WC1B 4HP
www.constablerobinson.com

First published in the UK by How To Books,
an imprint of Constable & Robinson Ltd., 2013

ISBN 978-1-8452-8510-4 (paperback)
ISBN 978-1-4721-1006-0 (ebook)

Printed and bound by CPI Group (UK) Ltd, Croydon, CR0 4YY

1 3 5 7 9 10 8 6 4 2

Acknowledgements

Thanks to all the dogs I have known and loved who continue to teach me so much.

Thanks also to Lesley Harris APDL for her endless patience – she listened, she read and she commented and helped make valid points readable and understandable.

Thank you also to Nikki and Giles at How To Books; Jo Stansall at Constable & Robinson; and Jon Davies.

Finally, thank you to Paul Manktelow for writing the foreword to this book.

Contents

Preface

Our modern-day dog's ancestor is the wolf – they share almost identical DNA so present many similar behaviours. However, our domestic dogs have evolved to live with humans and, because of this, now show many different behaviours compared with their wild cousins. With this in mind, the behaviour of wild wolves is not the focus of our attention here, but it has an important part to play in our learning. If we just looked to wolves, it would be like studying chimps in order to make sense of humans. They have their similarities but also their differences, so it is very useful to look at both for an understanding of how the communication works as well as behaviours, and therefore logical to look to wolves to gain some insight regarding their communication and how they work as a team.

It's interesting to speculate as to how wolves eventually evolved into what we now know as dogs. The human race began domesticating wolves thousands of years ago. Recent studies in Russia have revealed how this was probably done. They used the silver fox, an animal famed for its aggressive temperament, and picked the calmer and more placid pups. Within three generations, they found they were producing foxes that were able to interact with humans. Even more amazing was the fact that not only had they produced a gentler personality but that physical changes were happening, too, both in colour and general appearance – some animals having floppy ears, for instance. This almost certainly happened with the wolf as the brighter ones realised that there was a food source available if they hung around human settlements. Both sides of the partnership benefited: the wolves through food, and the humans by early warning and protection and, subsequently, by working together when hunting. As the changes in the wolves' colours and body shape occurred naturally, we humans would no doubt have hurried things along by encouraging the changes we liked.

As a result, vastly different looks appeared, culminating in the huge variety of domestic dogs we have today. So, in essence, we have different looks and kinder (as perceived by humans) personalities, but the brain make-up and communication skills remain the same.

Within our human family, we have to set boundaries. It is the same within a pack of dogs and, remember, the term 'pack' is a word devised by humans to describe a family of dogs or wolves, as 'pride' describes a family of lions. Within all these families, if there were no rules, boundaries, guidance or understanding then the group would not function adequately and therefore their survival would be compromised. We need to understand the domestic dog to understand fully their communication skills, their social behaviours and hierarchy. But similarly, they need to understand us as well – it is a two-way street.

Domestic dogs have the capacity to understand us to a certain extent – more so even than chimps, which are thought to be our closest relatives – but we must be aware that within each breed and litter there are many personalities just as there are in the human family.

This is what we work with – individual personalities. As with teaching anyone, how easily the student will learn depends largely on personality and intelligence. If the dog thinks the teacher is not up to the job, then learning will be limited.

We must clearly understand that a dog can only be a dog and a human a human; we both have to find a mutually acceptable level of understanding to enable the dog to adapt to the behaviours that we hope to see demonstrated.

In order to build the best possible relationship between dog and human, it is essential to avoid cruel behaviours and gadgets. Collars and leads are used because the law requires us to, but it is preferential to use a harness, particularly when working with a dog that has been abused and is spooked by restrictions around the back of the neck or around the throat. All you need are a lead, collar or Happy At Heel Harness (designed and patented by us), some toys, food rewards, kindness, consistency and imagination.

It's not what you say, it's what you do ... and it's not only what you do, it's what you feel. It all starts within you. So if your dog just isn't getting it, look at your own behaviour first – don't blame your dog.

The principles of PURE dog listening are nothing new; it is the language of the canine. Other people have written their take on communicating in such a way and so I thought now it was my turn. I have spent a considerable amount of time dog watching, reading and testing my theories and those of others, principally in the area of guiding and bringing up your dog without resorting to command training or bribing or using intimidating body language or vocals. Books written by John Fisher, Desmond Morris and Turid Rugaas were a huge inspiration early on. I have watched hundreds of people over the years with their dogs and children, working out why some were great and relaxed, some like cats on hot bricks, others completely oblivious to their owners while others were all over them like a rash. It was the owners that caught my imagination, and the more I spoke and asked them what they did, the more it dawned on me that less is more. Don't bug, don't bribe, don't intimidate – just guide in a gentle and consistent manner that they understand. When a dog is doing something 'naughty', it's because it doesn't get it.

I continue to spend time studying working dogs and pet dogs in kennels, family homes and professional environments, but wherever I meet them, the road of learning is never complete.

So in the words of Ignacio Estrada:

> *If the pupil will not learn the way we teach,*
> *then we will teach the way the pupil will learn.*

There are other people calling themselves dog listeners out there. So to stand out, I came up with 'PURE', which to me means staying natural and as close to canine communication as possible. It means applying a holistic approach to every aspect of the dog's world. My aim with this group is to keep it small and intimate so everyone is giving the same message to a very high standard. We know each other very well and continue to learn and discuss as we move forward. The group of PURE Dog Listeners not only conduct one-to-one consultations but also give their time up to help various charities for the benefit of dogs generally, and to enrich their own personal development as PURE Dog Listeners.

When we talk of 'traditional' trainers, the word 'traditional' is rather misleading – 'traditional' as in 'We've always done it that way'. But we're communicating with a different species, the canine, and they've never 'done it that way'. They've got their own way of doing things that has served them very well for thousands of years.

I like to think of this method of PURE Dog Listening as grassroots training or, more specifically, guidance in growing up, guidance in good manners and how your dog can fit into your life, stress free.

Foreword

As a vet in practice we see a great variety of dogs – big and small, tall and short, hairy and hairless, among countless other breed-distinguishing features. All of these blend into insignificance when we consider the variety of canine personalities we encounter. In the ten or so minutes spent in the consult room with a dog and owner, a surprising amount of information can be gathered about a dog's behaviour, an owner's behaviour and, most importantly, how the two interact with each other.

Some owners bring along their beloved pet on whom they obviously dote, showering it in affection on the consult table, yet the dog seems to ignore their every word and action. On the flip side of the coin we have another type of owner, similarly besotted with their dog, but in a quiet and understated way. Their dog appears to listen to their every command, trust their judgement and watch them to see if the 'nasty vet' approaching with a thermometer should be trusted or not. How can two owners and their soul mates have such contrasting relationships?

From a purely selfish point of view, I like nothing more than an obedient, friendly and cooperative pet in the consult room. From an owner's perspective, I can see no downsides to this either. A dog is our best friend, and we should treat them as such; if this is done correctly, your dog will give the same affection back to you. Now comes the tricky part: how do we go about teaching such behaviour?

Dog behaviour is one of the most complex aspects of veterinary practice. There are countless textbooks that can teach us as vets to do the most complex surgeries step-by-step, but some vets faced with even the simplest behavioural issues may be flummoxed. Owners and vets need not fear though – help is at hand. If you want a calm, well-rounded, loving and trusting dog, who listens and responds to your requests because he wants to, not because he has to, you have to have *two* vital things. First and most important, you need willpower, perseverance – no matter what – and commitment…and you will reach your goal.

The second thing? Well, you've already sorted that one. You've got this book in your hand. Read on and enjoy, and that goes for you *and* your dog.

Paul Manktelow BVMS MSc MRCVS

Introduction

Most dog owners don't want Lassie, Rin Tin Tin or Wonder Dog – they want a friend, a dog that walks nicely on the lead, that comes back when called, is non-aggressive and is generally well behaved. One that will be accepted anywhere and will not be an embarrassment. In short, a dog they can enjoy.

This book will help you gain a better understanding of why your dog does what it does and for you to be able to put into practice this method in order to correct undesirable behaviour in your own dog. Dogs communicate with body language and, in everything they do, there is a message. They are not naughty, they are trying to tell you something or get you to do something or they are just plain confused.

We're talking about a friendship here, one that is built on love and trust. Friends do not control one another by using force, intimidation or bribery or any other way for that matter. Why then should we rely on these methods when getting a dog to respond to us? I want my dog to love me, not fear me, and for both of us to enjoy a mutual respect.

So I neither want to force nor bribe my dog. I need my dog to relax and live as a natural thinking being, using its brain to work out how, when and where, not waiting to perform a programmed response for every move.

It never really matters what your dog does, it is what you do in response that is most important. And that's the focus of the training in this book.

Dogs are very intelligent animals, and it will become even clearer just how intelligent they are as you read through each chapter. So let's explore their psyche as deeply as we can, and try to see the world from their point of view.

To help us on the way, here's a thought-provoking, poetic perspective from Lesley Harris:

I am a Dog

I am a dog, and that's all I can be,
  But it COULD be so much if – just once – you could see
The world as it looks from a dog's point of view,
  The strange noises you make, the strange things that you do
We cannot understand and it causes us pain,
  But we TRY to be 'good' – then you're angry again.
We never do things 'to just get you mad',
  If you're angry with us, then it DOES make us sad.
Your world is not ours, and try as we may,
  We cannot understand 'every word that you say'.
We cherish our laws, they are honest and true,
  And perhaps there's a way we can teach them to you.
If you COULD find a way where you understand US,
  And then show what you want without making a fuss
We would be SO content, and we would serve you well –
  And we would be SO glad to be freed from our hell.

You never can know the deep stress that we bear,
  In a world where we feel there is no one to care.
A dog does not have a bad bone when he's born –
  It is humans who mould him, it is humans who form.
We chose to be with you, when once long ago,
  We left the wild places – so don't bring us low.
We cherish your friendship; we don't want to be slaves –
  Your dog looks to YOU to guide how he behaves.
So give the right signals to show what you need,
  We don't seek to try you – we want to pay heed.
Please learn how to guide us, to show us you care,
  And together – as friends – we've a whole world to share.

Lesley Harris

A Dog's Perspective – An Introduction by Spot

Hello. I'm Spot and I'm a dog. Just that…a dog. I won't tell you what breed I am because then you'll expect me to behave in a particular 'breed specific' way. So I'm just a dog.

I was one of a litter of seven. I had three brothers and three sisters and we were brought up by our mum. She was lovely, a good parent. We never knew our father – we've been told that he just turned up one night and left in the morning, never to be seen again. We were born sixty-four days later.

We stayed with Mum for eight weeks and it was a very important time. She taught us as much as she could about how to behave and taught us to be thoughtful of others and not bite hard. Between me and my brothers and sisters we tumbled and played and bit and growled and generally had lots of fun. Mind you, if I bit too hard the others would squeal and not play with me for a while. It wasn't fun being 'Billy No Mates'. I won't do that again.

Of course, at that time we didn't know we would be leaving. We thought that we'd all be staying together. But no, I think my mother had had enough of all seven of us after two months.

Mum had help from her human to look after us. The human fed my mum and, as we got older, Mum disappeared for a bit every now and again and the human would give us food, too. We'd tasted that food before – when we jumped up and licked Mum's lips, she would bring some of her food back up for us to eat. It was so yummy and warm and delicious.

We tried the same tactics with the human when she sat on the floor to be with us, but she didn't seem to like us licking her face. Every time we tried, jumping at her when she came in, but we couldn't reach her face...too high up on those legs! She told us to get down, and then bent down so her face was closer, but still she didn't produce her breakfast like Mum had.

One morning it got very noisy with lots of humans looking at us and pointing. They come in different shapes and sizes. Mum explained that they are called 'men' and 'women' and their puppies are called 'children' and come in two models: boys and girls. I didn't like this at all. The humans made lots of loud, strange noises and were leaning all over us. They picked me up and pushed their faces right up to mine. They kept making eye contact, which to a puppy is very scary.

My brother Rex had some humans looking at him, too. They were much more thoughtful, sitting near Rex but not putting any pressure on him. He was able to go up to them when he felt able. They outstretched their arms so Rex could sniff them; he liked their smell and then, seeing that they were lovely, crawled up for a cuddle.

They just waited for him to realise that they weren't a threat. I wish they'd told the humans with me the best way to behave. Suddenly it *was all over. I was parted from my mum and brothers and sisters. I was taken by a man and a woman with a boy and a girl. I was really frightened. They took me to a new place full of strange sights, sounds and, of course, smells. I was nervous and soon added my own smell to let them know I'd arrived. The humans got very angry. They shouted at me and rubbed my nose in the area where I'd marked.*

I cried all night. I missed my mum and my brothers and sisters. I was in a room on my own now with a very big bed . . . a big, empty bed!

They do a lot of this shouting and general noise-making. It seems to be the way they communicate with one another. They've tried it on me but I just don't understand and then they get angry again. Sometimes they tap me on the nose or bottom or shake me and then they might pick me up and try to be my friend. I'm just so confused; the rules keep changing. They give me a biscuit from a plate on the table. That's nice, but when I help myself to another, they shout at me.

They keep calling my name but, when I respond, they don't do anything.

'Spot . . . Spot . . . Spot . . . Spot . . .'

If I could, I'd say to them, 'Yes, I know what my name is. What do you want?' I've also worked out that a few of their sounds have some meaning, such as my name. I know what 'Sit' means because they say it very sharply and force my backside down. They seem to think the louder the sound is, the more I'll understand.

I know that they're not bad people and that most of the time they are kind but they just seem to think that I should understand these funny noises they make. They lead very complicated lives but, as I said earlier, I'm just a dog, an uncomplicated animal, and as long as I've got some food, know how to get some more, have time to play, have someone who'll know what to do if things get scary and be really sure where I fit into the scheme of things, then I'd be happy.

My humans took me to a strange place called 'the vet'. (I call them 'my humans' because, although they are completely disorganised, I've become very fond of them.) After the vet visit my humans took me out from our den for the first time and, for some reason, they tied me to them with a tether of some sort from my collar to their hand.

I was a bit wary at first but soon started to enjoy it. I pulled to see what was around the next corner, loads of great smells and – whoooooosh! – a fast, shiny thing raced by. Lucky it didn't hit us. I barked at it and it sped off. Great job – one bark and they run away.

There was another dog – well, it smelt like a dog – he was massive and barking at me. I was a bit scared and tried to hide behind my humans. They picked me up and took me over to this dog to say hello. What do they think they're doing? I'm terrified, I don't know him, he may eat me or lick me to death. Why couldn't I just look at him from a distance and then get closer if I felt OK about it?

As I told you, I'm just a dog and live a very simple life. I'm really good at being a dog, it's probably my best asset. I am, however, really bad at being a human, but that's the way my humans seem to think I should act.

The problem is that I don't understand the human world; there are loads of strange and scary sights and sounds when we leave the den. Big, noisy, metal boxes on wheels that are fast and come very close. I jump up at them to chase them away but get told off. I jump up at my humans to ask for help, to ask for a decision, but they tell me off. How am I supposed make them understand that I'm scared sometimes?

We then get to a big space and my human unties me. Wow, what a lovely feeling... I'm free and can run around and have fun. What's that over there? It's a squirrel. Game on! Off I go, I'll soon have lunch sorted and be very popular. My humans are making a lot of noise but, instead of standing back there making a lot of fuss, they should be over here backing me up. Look, I know it's not a herd of buffalo, but it's still hard to surround a squirrel on my own, particularly if he's up a tree throwing nuts at me. Because of the lack of support, the squirrel escaped but, hey ho, some you win...

On my way back to my pack – still being very noisy – I find a nice, really ripe, dead rabbit. That'll do! If we can't have squirrel stew, perhaps they'll like rabbit ragout. As I approach them with my prize, they look both angry and horrified. When I push the rabbit into their groins, they are quite unappreciative of my gift.

They took me to a place called 'Obedience Class', which I found rather confusing. Although I now realise there are some really good ones, the class I attended seemed a bit pointless to me. It appears that to humans it is vital that their dog goes to the village hall every Thursday evening and walks around in a circle for an hour in the company of some other dogs before going home again. Strange creatures these humans, aren't they? I don't know any of these dogs, they're not from my pack. Some are all right but others are trouble-makers or just confused.

As the days went by, I started to understand more of the sounds that humans make and tried my hardest to do things they ask. I walk close on walks, I sit when they ask, and go to my bed. I still chase things out and about – it's fun and I feel free, even if I do get a stern telling off when I get back. Surely one day they will be pleased with what I have brought back to eat.

I felt they needed me to do more, so I let them know when there is a knock at the door or if something is outside and I can hear it. I shout to let them know and they shout, too. I've alerted them to danger and they are now joining in. Great!

Oh...not so great. They are now shouting at me, panicking, so I'll shout louder. Do they want me to shout more? I don't know – I'm so confused – but what I do know is that I'm frightened and they are frightened. What should we all do? They are doing nothing. Do they *want me to do something? Bite? Run away? Why can't they make a clear decision? Is that why I'm here maybe? No, don't expect me to come up with the answer...please.*

I can't relax during the day, not knowing what is going to happen or what they are going to do. I can't eat my food in the morning as I'm rather on edge. What will today bring? I follow them wherever they go in the house. I hate being on my own and I don't think my human does either because they always need me with them. Yes, they do...I'm sure they do.

I sit close and lean on them when we are in the den; they seem to like the reassurance that I'm there to protect them. See, I do fit in, but it's a hard job. I've always got to be alert and don't really relax until the evening when we are all in and they unwind in front of this weird wobbly box that booms out strange sounds. I hate it and shout now and again when it is on. Not sure what it is, but it knows if it tries anything on, I'm the one it will have to deal with. Not that I'll have a clue what to do...but I have warned it. I hit it once and my humans hit me and shouted at me. I won't do that again. I still hate it, though, and have to be alert just in case.

When they sleep, I can sleep, too. But like any good parent, I'll be there for them. That's what they want, I'm sure.

We go for nice walks now on the lead. I've learnt to stay by their sides, unless, of course, there is something more exciting (which there generally is), or I think something may be a problem, and I need to bark to tell it to go away. I did that to a wheelie bin last week, but it didn't move. Seemed odd. It's got wheels! Anyway, I bit it as we walked past. That'll teach it! But I don't understand them in the slightest. However, I have food and a bed and we play games and do lots of stuff I enjoy.

One day when I was out for my walk, who should I bump into but my brother Rex. We had a great time racing around and catching up on old times. You remember I told you how different the humans who took Rex were to the pack that I joined? Well, Rex has really landed on his paws. I love my humans to bits but they drive me crazy with their inconsistency. They try hard but, just as we seem to be getting somewhere, they get it wrong again. They are kind, caring... but so confused.

Rex tells me that from day one his humans never told him to do something he didn't understand; they showed him instead. They didn't keep talking at him in a language he didn't understand but communicated with a lot of non-verbal signals. 'Body language' I think the humans call it. As a result, when Rex is spoken to by his human, it's always good stuff: 'Fetch'... 'Come'... 'Good boy'. And so when Rex hears his name called, his response is: 'What can I do for you?' When I hear my name called, I always feel a bit worried that I won't know what is expected of me.

It seems that Rex's owner talked to something called a 'PURE Dog Listener' and got lots of advice and information from them which made life so much easier for both Rex and his human. The good news is that we often meet at the park now and, while Rex and I play, our humans talk. Rex's human has started telling mine about the techniques he used and things are looking promising. Each time I come back from playtime with Rex, my human is just that little bit more switched on. We may be getting somewhere. Watch this space!

Three Years Later

I'm now three years old, life is good and I still see my brother Rex from time to time; we have great fun. However, what a surprise! I met my sister Spotless on a walk the other day in the woods as I was playing with my human. I recognised her immediately; she looks very much like me but has no spots! She is not a girly girl and doesn't live up to her name, as she is generally covered in mud.

She was much less relaxed than either Rex or me, so once we'd sorted out the usual polite greetings, a bit of rear-end sniffing and the like, she opened up a little. She'd gone to a home when we all left our mum, but at the age of eight months she suddenly found herself being driven to a kennel and left there. She didn't know why.

Spotless said she'd been a perfect girl at home, barking all the time in the house when people knocked at the door, barking at cats to keep them away from the garden, and she even burrowed under the fence to next door and brought back a rabbit that was just sitting on the patio. Actually, barking at the cats was fun, and although they really annoyed her, it gave her something to think about.

She'd been on walks and chased and caught the odd rabbit, which was pretty difficult as they are very fast. So when one arrived next door she reasoned it was an easy dinner for the family and everyone would be happy. Sadly, that was not the case. Everyone shouted at her and then the neighbour came round, who up until then had been OK. Oh dear, not happy at all. When he left, she was told off again. They obviously don't like the neighbour now, but she doesn't know why.

Spotless said she jumped up on all the family and visitors alike. She always got attention when she asked for it; sometimes they were grumpy, sometimes nice…no idea why. Very confusing though! Spotless wasn't sure about strangers and her anxiety made her even more jumpy until one day, she had had enough and nipped one of them. Then her owner held her down and shouted…she was scared and trapped. Then there was another scary visitor and he bent down to stroke her, so she growled. But he still carried on and put his hand out to stroke her. She couldn't get away so she gave him a little nip. Now that wasn't something her humans seemed very pleased about. If only they had told the person to stop, she wouldn't have had to go that far. She was frightened, so what's a girl supposed to do in that situation?

She was sent away to this kennel and, lo and behold, who should choose to take her home but a friend of Rex's humans. She now realises that all the things she'd done were a bit over the top. She was making decisions for her family that really weren't necessary. If only they had shown her how they wanted her to be. They were so intense all the time she didn't have the space to think and relax.

Her human has sensitively given her time to ease up and enjoy the simple things in life. The great thing now is that when she barks, her owner goes over to the window and looks out and then gently moves her away from the loud banging and holds her softly. That gives her time to feel his calmness and it helped her to understand quickly that he liked her bark, but then kindly accepted the fact that she was upset and showed her that all was OK. It's great that someone understands her now and she is beginning to chill out.

Her walks used to be a nightmare on the lead – 'tug of war' comes to mind – how I used to be when I was younger. Now she is learning to walk with, and enjoy being with her kind, understanding human because she is beginning to trust. If she is worried, then he will take the right action to show her all is fine and that he makes the decisions in her life. She adores him, but more than that now – she also trusts and respects him.

It was great when she was first taken from the kennels. He just let her settle in her own time, he didn't pressurise her into meeting loads of new people and going to loads of strange places. He let her spend some time in her new home so she could enjoy just being a dog, get to know her new human and how to behave around the home and garden.

Spotless said she was actually able to sleep really well after a week during the day and started to relax and enjoy being herself. OK, she still gets stuff wrong, but whenever she does, her human just gently puts her right. She has learnt to control her excitable jumping up, as she gets a cuddle if she doesn't jump, so instead she stands back and waits patiently. She doesn't get upset or hyped up so easily now either; she doesn't feel the need to bite as he is always there making sure no one backs her into a situation which unsettles her.

Anyway, I'd better stop now. As you hear more about how we think and what we'd like from our humans, you'll hopefully understand that all we want is to be loved and understood and, above all, to be able to understand you!

Oh yes, before I go, the coolest thing ever happened last week. Rex and Spotless came to stay for two nights. We had such fun, eventually knocking over a plant pot in the sitting room, but hey, Bob, my human, didn't fret. He just cleared it up in our view, and said nothing... although I know now when he says nothing it means he's not at all happy. I'll be more careful in future... best play outside.

Life is so gooooooood!

1

Understanding Your Dog

Anthropomorphism – Dogs as Humans

For most training methods, anthropomorphism is a cardinal sin – and to a certain extent this is valid. Dogs will never be 'humans in furry coats', and it is not always helpful to apply our human characteristics to them. However, both species do share fundamental needs. All animals need food; all need to feel safe and secure; all have the desire to procreate; all will protect their young with their lives; all have evolved in the most appropriate way to live comfortably in their chosen environment; all will fight by whatever means available for their survival... and all need to relax and have fun.

Very young children display these common traits to perfection. Neither dogs nor toddlers have any concept of right or wrong, good or bad, kind or cruel, honest or dishonest – they just do what it takes for their own survival.

With children, we understand this and encourage and teach in a very gentle and age-appropriate way. We do not bark commands at them, we do not punish them for not understanding, we show them by example how we want them to behave, where the boundaries lie, what it takes to fit in and thrive in their world, until they reach an age where they can understand what is required and start to make the right choices for themselves. Even then, because we have shown them that we are to be trusted to make all the good decisions, they will naturally look to their parent as a source of safety and learning whenever they are unsure of how to act.

Children have the advantage of, first, being human; second, they have the ability to understand the spoken word in a way that dogs never will; and third, they have a much more complex brain which is able to reason, understand past, present and future actions or planned actions, and the likely consequences of their deeds. By the age of around three, they can begin to understand what is expected of them in terms of behaviour.

Dogs cannot develop understanding in the same way, so we need to adapt our training and nurturing to make it dog-specific. They are a different species living in an alien world, unable to understand why we give signals which are often diametrically opposed to those which are hard-wired into their canine psyche. They cannot understand more than a few words of our language, so every bit as much as tiny children, they need a human who understands what it takes to make them feel safe and secure.

Humans and dogs may react best to different approaches, but their needs are similar. You take the time and trouble to find what works for your child – so do the same for your dog.

Dogs are amazingly adaptable; they usually, somehow, manage to fit into a world which makes little sense to them – as long as they live with kind, if ignorant, humans! The unlucky ones do not get even this help – they are beaten for doing wrong, and shouted at for not understanding. More often than not, the focus is on punishing them for *not* doing as the human wishes, but they're never shown in a kind and patient way what the human *does* require from them. They can often end up aggressive, shut down, or just generally an emotional mess.

In a natural or 'wild' environment, canines have evolved to survive very successfully. They have a set of rules by which they live, mainly non-verbal, using body language which all canines understand perfectly. They have developed a way of doing things that enables them to exist perfectly in their physical environment.

Language and Relationships

No dog wakes up in the morning and thinks, 'My mission today is to annoy my human.' We do not believe for one moment that most dogs try to take control, be the Alpha or the leader. They are clever and learn how to read us, how to manipulate us and train us. They ask questions in the only way they know how and, if we give out the wrong signals, they get it wrong through no fault of their own. They are just being dogs and asking how to fit in.

How our dogs behave is up to us. If you get it wrong, don't worry – you can change it. By changing your behaviour towards your dog, you will then change your dog's behaviour towards you and others.

It's important to remember that all problems with your dog boil down to a communication issue. You are talking a language they don't understand, and they are talking a language you don't understand. It has to be the responsibility of the more adaptable party – with the capacity to be proactive, not reactive, and also with the capacity to think logically – to learn the language of the dog to understand what is going on in its mind. You need to become bilingual, and so does your dog. Then there will be harmony, and each will be able to understand what is expected of the other. It is not just down to who feeds and walks your dog – if only it were that easy! It runs far deeper than that. It's how you respond in a way the dog can understand. You have to show them you respect their ways and their instincts and work with those instincts, not against them, to bring harmony to the relationship.

And that's the key word – 'relationship'. Just as in your relationships with other humans – whether friends or loved ones – it's a two-way street. You need to make your contribution to the relationship every day. We've all seen what happens when one side of a partnership decides they don't have to make an effort. And as before, it never really matters what your dog does, it matters more how you respond to those actions.

The Survival Instinct in a Human World

To a dog, everything is about survival – not only theirs but the whole family's as well. Everything is subordinated to the survival of the family and, if you look at your own family, the same goes for us, too. Nothing else matters. All canines approach this with the same attitude, whether one of the Queen's corgis, a Hollywood starlet's 'handbag dog', a rough sleeper's crossbreed or your family pet. Dogs are programmed by thousands of years of evolution to survive as we did.

Most dogs if abandoned in the New Forest would survive – they would quickly realise that their human isn't going to turn up with their food. The dog would seamlessly slip into survival mode and would hunt and scavenge to survive. It might even join up with other dogs to form a mutually supportive pack. We as humans in the Western world would struggle; it's not easy to live without all our gadgets and comforts. We have lost so many skills and rely on too many easy options.

The world we live in is completely alien to the dog – they do not understand about locks on our doors and that others in close proximity are generally not a threat. In our community structures we tend to live close to our neighbours, which can be unsettling for some dogs. Because nowadays our dogs do not roam freely like they did fifty years ago, many become territorial. We're not in and out of our neighbours' houses, as many of us don't even know our neighbours these days, so in recent times the dog's world has become ever more insular and scary. They are not able or free to roam and run from fearful things when they need to, or take things at their own pace. We pressurise them to conform to our society unlike any other animal we have domesticated.

It is too much to expect other species to understand the world we now live in; it is for us to adapt our communication skills to show them that we are in control and they are safe in our hands – that the protection of the pack or family is our responsibility. We are the decision-makers and can therefore relieve them of pressure. We have to show the dog that we will also be there to lead them and they just have to follow. If we give them this assurance, then they will relax by our side in the knowledge that they are protected and safe. We can then take responsibility for those situations which they do not understand, they're frightened of or which they don't have the skills to deal with, in a way that's acceptable in our society.

PURE Dog Listening

PURE Dog Listening provides a method for life which needs to be adopted as an ongoing process by the whole family. Be the decision-maker for your dog. Remember, like a company director, a parent or carer, they never have a day off. You are always the decision-maker/leader providing ground rules and boundaries. The process will become second nature and enables further advanced training to take place in a stress-free environment.

As with learning any new skill, you will at times make mistakes. Remember when you learnt to drive? If you do get something wrong, don't beat yourself up and think that it's the end of the world, but learn from the experience. If you notice another family member 'getting it wrong', point it out to them but don't be tempted to treat this as a point-scoring exercise. In the same vein, should you slip up and have it pointed out, try not to get defensive; take note and move forward. The aim is to have a happy and well-balanced dog, so let's try to leave our egos to one side while practising.

You will, I hope, follow this method and have a truly wonderful relationship with your dog because, for the first time, you will really understand it.

Body Language

We know dogs don't talk. Maybe they utter the odd bark, howl or make comfortable contented noises, but the bulk of their communication is through body language. We, too, communicate a lot with both conscious and subconscious body language. If the words don't match the body language then we become unbelievable and untrustworthy, and we pick up on these 'tells' instinctively.

While dogs can't talk, they do, though, have an ability to understand some of our spoken words. And they are real experts in picking up and interpreting our body language, whether for good or ill. If you unwittingly give your dog an incorrect signal, don't be surprised if it behaves in a way that you find unacceptable. You *told* your dog to do it, or at the very least signalled that it was all right to do it. Let's show them how we wish them to behave, how to fit in. We cannot tell them by using words or bullying them, and we cannot expect respect if we do not show them respect, or if we try to dominate them. We have to show them in a caring way what is acceptable and what is not. Effectively, we need to lead by example. Be kind, considerate and patient with dogs and people alike, and you will reap the rewards. Be a bully or expect all cultures and species to learn our language, and you have set yourself up for failure.

If you don't want to fail your dog, learn his body language so you understand what he is thinking when undesirable behaviour appears. It's also important to be able to ascertain whether your dog is relaxed and happy. It's true that a lot of what we have learnt about dogs is from observing wolves and other canines in the wild and domestic situations. But we can also look at our own behaviour as well, and see how we react in similar situations when we are under pressure or stressed. The difference is that we can be proactive if we think and reason, then come to a logical conclusion before we react.

Dogs understand their own body language. We have many different breeds out there and they are not there through natural selection; we have selectively bred to all different shapes and sizes. What we have not changed is the brain make-up. They all think the same – who's protector and who's provider? – as we do, too. Different breeds tend towards different behavioural issues, but it is all for the same reasons. It is also true to say that any breed, any age can display any behavioural problem. Dogs will want to know: 'Who can I count on?' … 'Am I safe?' … and 'Can it eat me or can I eat it?'

Eye contact is another essential element of dogs' body language that it is really important to understand. In essence, canines do not make eye contact with one another until they want to interact, and then it will not be prolonged eye contact, unless for the purposes of a heated discussion or play. In many ways, this is similar to human interaction, so we shouldn't be surprised our intense, sustained eye contact may provoke an unwanted reaction, rather than prevent it. I have included a guide to this on p. 68.

Trust and Respect

The 'Sit', 'Stay', 'Heel' and 'Come' are important in our world – but I've never seen a dog ask another to do any of these acts. They have to be carefully taught, and built on a foundation of trust and respect.

The basic commands are the skills we humans need to teach to pass canine obedience tests, but you don't have to be a control freak. Don't try to micro-manage every action of your dog's life. It's important to have a dog that will follow these simple requests, but it's best achieved through cooperation. In order to teach these exercises in any environment, your dog needs to choose their teacher as the one they ultimately trust and feel safe with. That person should be the one with whom a dog can relax and learn, and who enables understanding in a mutually beneficial way.

We understand what a dog is thinking by its reactions. A dog is a dog at the end of the day, as we are all humans. It is also true that certain breeds tend to display different behaviours, because we humans have tinkered with nature and produced retrievers, herders, guarders, hunters, terriers, and so on. The list is endless. They are all dogs, but may also have a bolted-on retrieving or herding instinct enhanced by human intervention with breeding. When it really matters, those additional behaviours drop away, and the dog reverts to pure canine survival. To train dogs effectively, we look beyond the breed to the individual personalities of each dog. It's worth remembering that there are shy guard dogs, aggressive lap dogs and everything in between.

Different people react to situations depending on personality and upbringing. Why should other species be any different? We must let a dog be just that – a dog. We bring it up gently with boundaries, consistency and love. There are no tricks. It is straightforward if you open your mind to learning. This is the way we used to be with dogs before we brought them into our homes and they had no specific job but just to be there for us. So we have essentially 'humanised' them and they are there for us and our emotional needs...which is where it goes so wrong for them.

I am not saying you can't love your dog, cuddle your dog, kiss it or have it on your bed. The ground rules in your house are the ones that you set. It's your house, your dog, your rules. The only rule that you must always adhere to in order to ensure a harmonious relationship is that your dog works around you, not you around your dog. You can have as much interaction as you want, possibly more than you do now, because it will be on your terms. In essence, make sure it is you who calls a dog into your space; don't let the dog call the shots. Movement is powerful – teach your dog to come to you, then you have set the ground rules around who is training whom.

In the case of 'assistance' dogs, who enable people to lead independent lives, they do help us but they are given 'games' to play that are rewarded. These games might involve teaching how to switch on a light, helping someone get dressed, guiding someone...those tasks have to be enjoyable and taught in such a way that dogs can accomplish them perfectly. But those dogs also need to have time off duty when they can just be themselves. Like us, they also need to have a work–life balance.

Pet dogs need stimulation, too – team-building games and fun walks – and time to rest, sniff and play in peace and quiet. In essence, they need 'dog time' to be themselves. To be able to enjoy a game, a dog needs to be relaxed, but some dogs won't play or can't play. Apart from the older, infirm dogs, or ill dogs for that matter, the main reason a dog won't play is that either they are rather stressed or it is too preoccupied with looking out for you, itself and the rest of the family.

Kindness, Empathy and Guidance

The method used in this book is based on kindness, empathy and guidance. It provides a holistic approach to creating a calm and happy dog owner, who:

- Is proactive and teaches dogs to self-control.
- Is non-aggressive and only uses appropriate correction.
- Does not have to resort to intimidation, drugs or cruel gadgets.
- Is able to utilise a dog's natural instincts and language.

This method is based on understanding dogs and their natural behaviour and needs a sense of calm, consistency, empathy, patience and a positive mental attitude. It will really work if you are dedicated.

The PURE Dog Listening method will not:

- Enforce your will on your dog.
- Turn dogs into robots.
- Offer a quick fix without effort on the part of the owner (there is no fixed time frame).

It's also worth remembering that this approach is not a way of dominating your dog, ignoring it or being cruel in any shape or form. With this in mind, you should always avoid:

- Teasing with food.
- Clicking your fingers.
- Poking your dog in the ribs.
- Forcing your dog to 'confront its fear'.
- Exhausting your dog so it sleeps.

This is the basis of my teaching, and one that we need to make absolutely clear to all dog owners who would like to use this approach to build better relationships with their dogs.

Five to Thrive – The Behavioural Cycle

The Five to Thrive diagram below is our framework, our starting point. You will see that all your dog's behaviour issues slot into any one or more of these five areas.

THE FIVE TO THRIVE BEHAVIOURAL CYCLE

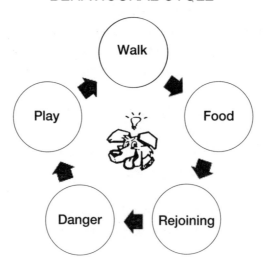

Dogs' behavioural problems crop up in any one or more of these areas. Interestingly enough, in many cases if you do not address all five areas, then the problem you solved in one area may rear its ugly head in another area in a different way. So to leave out one area is like talking gibberish. To be completely convincing, you really need to use this as a constant in your home with your dog; it's the way to communicate clearly and consistently. Imagine talking Russian to an Englishman, then realising he speaks English, so you switch to English...then a few weeks down the line you start talking Russian again. Confusing?

It's also worth remembering – you're already dealing with situations such as feeding, walking, rejoining and playing with your dog. But it is *how* you do it that is most important.

Our goal is to have:

1. A patient dog during food preparation, who will eat enthusiastically at meal times rather than graze.

2. A stress-free walk with your dog on and off the lead.

3. A calm dog when we come home or have visitors – it is lovely to be welcomed home, but not mugged.

4. A gentle, quiet, confident and non-aggressive dog, confident in the knowledge that we will sort out the scary stuff.

5. A dog who will play with us, and enjoy being with us and our time together wherever we are.

Within the pages of this book you will learn to achieve all of the Five to Thrive principles, explain why your dog does what it does, and correct any behaviour problems. If you can understand the reasoning behind the solution, then you and your dog are much more likely to get a result.

Please note – in some cases, the cause of your dog's unaccep-table behaviour (such as aggression) could be due to a medical problem. If you're in doubt, it is always advisable to seek advice from a vet.

It is important to realise that this method is a way of life with your dog and it will become easier and second nature to you as you make progress. Like learning any language, it takes time and commitment. The first two to three weeks are always the hardest; there will be changes in your dog's behaviour – some good, some just different and some not as acceptable. In my view, all changes are 'good changes' as it means that you are getting through to your dog and it may again try to push the boundaries in another way. At this stage, you need to remain that true decision-maker and show your dog that this behaviour is not acceptable, and that other behaviours are preferred. Then you are on the road to educating your dog to fit in with you and your world.

It is imperative that you cover all of the elements of the Five to Thrive system. Every canine lives by those basic principles – all of them, all of the time. This ensures peace of mind and will reinforce you as the dog's guide through life. Only completing part of the method and expecting to succeed is like going to a driving school and telling them that you don't need to learn about braking, because you will be a careful driver. You can't expect to pass your test while lacking an essential foundation of driving knowledge. What would your chances be?

If your dog is not getting attention for doing something tried and tested, then it will try something else. If you cave in, then the dog will think, 'Ah-ha, you almost had me convinced, but you didn't come up to scratch there.' It is very important to remember to be patient, calm and understanding. You will have to show your dog many times in some instances what is correct and what is not – it won't be learnt in five seconds. So be patient and work with your dog and don't expect too much too soon. And it becomes easier if you don't think of having a 'problem' with your dog. Try to think of it more as a challenge and you will have a much greater chance of success.

This way of communicating is quite easy to learn and very soon you will be able to interpret what your dog is doing and therefore what it is saying. The difficult part is you changing to the new ways from your old ways. Be patient with yourself and your dog – it will happen.

Canines talk with their body language, and so must you for them to truly understand you. But this doesn't mean you simply putting your hand up for a 'Sit' as you go through a door. Dogs don't tell dogs to 'Sit'; they show them they have priority through their physical state as is explained later. If you've ever seen two dogs together, one always goes through the door first. It is not because they have made the other 'Sit' or 'Stay' – it is because they have earned respect. So please do not use 'Sit', 'Wait' and 'Stay' to interrupt unacceptable behaviour, or reward bad behaviour by redirecting your dog to a food reward of a bone or chew. Attention and rewards are not given for undesirable behaviour. You must remain calm and be your dog's guide.

2

Feeding

If you have more than one dog, you may well have noticed a variety of different behaviours at feeding time: one might stand back while the other eats and then starts its own; one may bolt down its food and then grab the other's; or there may be fights over food, whether it be a bowl of food, bones or chews. Others will all eat at the same time with no swapping and bullying, relaxed in the knowledge that there is no need for pushing and shoving and food stealing. In all these situations, the dogs are communicating how they feel, how they fit in and who has respect. It's all about who's in calm control.

You may as an owner have left a couple of treats for your dog when you went out and returned to find they were only eaten once you'd got back. Or have you ever wondered why some dogs may only eat in the evening and not the morning? Or why some dogs will take food treats and some won't? This behaviour is most commonly due to stress and anxiety, and how they are coping with their environment. (Unless, of course, there is a medical reason, often indicated by sudden onset.)

If your dog eats well, it means it is very well adjusted in this area. Eating 'well' means eating meals when offered, and taking food rewards wherever you are. But however well your dog eats, it's still important to understand the behavioural issues around food, as each element has a bearing on the others.

Good Feeding Habits

We use food as a reward intermittently for a job well done, but remember – if you do not phase it out, then the reward actually becomes a bribe and you will end up not being able to go anywhere without a sack of treats in your handbag as your dog will not do anything for you unless you have food readily available.

In the wild, a canine stomach when eating a natural diet is designed to digest huge quantities of food in one go. Conversely, dogs can also go for days or even longer without eating – and with no lack of performance. In fact, a canine is at its optimum with an empty stomach. However, because of the many different types of food we feed our dogs nowadays, the frequency and quantities given at each feed will vary. If you usually feed your dog once a day, initially try splitting the same quantity into two meals. This will give you two opportunities to display priority over feeding – showing your dog that you have control in a kind and gentle manner.

Try not to be too rigid with meal times, or you'll get a dog demanding to be fed because it's one minute past twelve, when you're right in the middle of doing something else. The change doesn't have to be great; sometimes just a change of routine will do. If you feed your dog first thing in the morning before your shower, then you could perhaps from time to time go to the kitchen, get yourself a drink, have a slice of toast, then feed it. Dogs are very good at picking up on our routines, so if you always stir your tea three times, then have a slice of toast before feeding your dog, then as you wipe the last crumb from your lips, it will be there demanding to be fed as the next action in the chain.

When the family eats, their dog should not be involved at all. But when we feed our dogs, it is vital that they understand that food comes courtesy of us and that they must be patient. And any family member in the house at feeding time should take part in the feeding as this will reinforce the dog's perception of who has control at feeding times.

Priority Feeding

Prepare your dog's food in full view of it. When it's ready, you have 'priority of feeding'. Together with the other family members present, pop a grape or similar sized morsel in your mouths and enjoy, with no eye contact with your dog. This shows that you're not making a big deal out of this exercise or offering a challenge. You must do this naturally. There should be no overdramatic 'Mmmmmm...this is the best grape I've ever had!'

It is also vital that there should be no teasing with food. Act as if you were cooking and just want to test the seasoning. As soon as you have finished your mouthful, place your dog's food on the floor (change the place sometimes to avoid being predictable), then walk a couple of paces and turn away from the dog without saying anything. By turning away, you are indicating that it is your dog's turn to eat, and that it can also eat in peace without being glared at, which could be interpreted as a challenge with you possibly wanting to take the food back.

Staying in Control

There is no need to get your dog to sit; a patient dog gets food when you are ready. Once you've given it the food, do not try to take it

away, as you could get bitten. For a dog, it is confusing to be given
something and then have it taken away.

Stay in the room while it is eating so you can you see what your
dog does without crowding it. The dog can only do one of four things:

1. It will go straight to its bowl and eat everything – i.e. 'wolf
    it down' – and this is the ideal. Again, born out of instinct, if
    danger were to threaten and it had to flee, there's now food
    in its belly and its chances of survival have increased. Dogs
    are also designed to take their food by bolting it down; they
    are not designed to graze.

2. It may glance at its food and walk away as if to say, 'Not
    bothered!' The message being given off is: 'Leave it there.
    When I want to then I'll eat, because I am the important one
    and I know that you won't touch it.' If there is another dog
    in the house, this is not generally an option.

3. It may go to the food bowl, eat a mouthful or two and then
    walk away. This option is very similar to option 2. It wants
    a food bowl down as a status symbol but is also a bit hungry
    so has a quick snack first.

4. Another option is the dog taking the food from the bowl,
    dropping it on the floor in front of the humans and then
    eating while trying to make eye contact. He may well take
    some and bury it in his bed for later to eat when you are
    around.

If your dog behaves in any of the ways other than the first, you
should pick up its bowl as soon as it is abandoned, and throw away

the unfinished food. It must not be fed again until the next mealtime – and that includes food rewards. Will it be hungry? Yes. Will it die? No. Will it have learnt a really valuable lesson? Yes. Even if it has used Option 1 and emptied its bowl, it still needs to be removed, cleaned and put out of sight. Even an empty food bowl can be used as a status symbol, with the dog potentially thinking: 'That's where I've trained my humans to deliver my food.' We often see dogs growling and guarding empty food bowls. Fresh water, of course, should be available at all times.

If your dog attempts to help load the dishwasher or beg or steal from the table, then guide it away – this is *your* food, and no one else's. Say nothing and it'll get the message. The trouble is, if you verbalise your feelings when you are trying to correct your dog, it'll still be doing it when it's twenty years old. If you say nothing, then the message will get through that you are not interested and, try as it might, it's not going to win attention by doing what you disapprove of.

Do remember, though, that if you walk away from your dinner at the table, what you are saying in canine terms is that you have finished your meal. So don't be tempted to show anger – try to be understanding and just guide him away, with no speech, no eye contact and no emotion.

My belief is that it's unnecessary to get your dog to sit or perform in any way for a meal. It should be an activity free from pressure. This is a human perception of control and there's no one better than us for needing to feel in control. And just to see what impact that has on us, try this simple exercise on your partner. Invite them to sit at the dining table, pour a glass of wine and bring in a beautifully cooked and presented meal. Carefully place the meal in front of your partner, wait for them to pick up their knife and fork and, just as they are about to lift the food to their mouth, say, 'Wait!' in a very firm voice. Keep them waiting thirty seconds or so, then give permission to eat.

If you want to up the ante with your partner a bit, you could remove the meal completely when they are only halfway through – that would make them respect you.

Or would it?

The Priority Feeding System

- The decision-maker eats first and controls feeding times.

- Do not incorporate your dog's feeding with your meals at the kitchen table. That will encourage begging.

- Prepare your dog's food and yours, and you eat your morcel of food first e.g. a grape. Then place your dog's food down. Say nothing.

- Turn and step away, but stay in the room. If you leave, your dog will more often than not follow you out, concerned as to your whereabouts.

- Remove the food bowl when your dog walks away, whether eaten or not.

- Make fresh water available all day.

- Follow these rules for a couple of weeks. It is a particularly useful method to bring back in if you have been away or are experiencing challenging behaviour.

Food Aggression and Advanced Priority Feeding

Some dogs are 'food aggressive' or have other serious problems around feeding. They may have been a rescue dog that previously had to fight for every mouthful or a dog that has been challenged or teased with food. You may never know the reason for acting in this way. Whatever the reason, it doesn't matter – you can make it better from this point on. With most food issues all will be resolved if you follow the Priority Feeding system detailed above. However, we always need a 'Plan B' for those times where 'Plan A' doesn't work. The following technique rarely has to be used, but when it is it sends an incredibly powerful message to the dog.

Feed the same amount as usual but split the food into three bowls. As with normal priority feeding, before you place the first food bowl down, you have your grape or biscuit. You only eat before the first food bowl. Put the bowl down, take a few steps away and then turn away (thereby avoiding offering a challenge when facing your dog).

As soon as that bowl is empty, put down bowl two some distance away and walk away, picking up the empty first bowl. When the dog has emptied bowl two, then bowl three goes down immediately, probably where you placed bowl one. You are not making a big deal of this but staying calm. You've eaten first and then shown in a calm, unhurried way you have the power over the food. The message you are giving your dog is: 'Now I've eaten, it's your turn. Here's some food…and some more…and some more. You don't need to get nasty over food because I will keep you supplied. I can look after you, and you can trust me to feed you.' You will be taking all the stress away from your dog and showing that you care and that food will be provided. There's now no need to become aggressive. You're also getting the dog to walk from bowl to bowl and thereby reinforcing your message through body language, which is a very authoritative act. Movement is a powerful tool.

Stopping Priority Feeding

Think of a child being taught to say 'Please' or 'Thank you'. Every time they are given something, they get a verbal prompt by the adult – 'Please' or 'Thank you' – followed by praise when they get it right. Once the child has learnt that good manners are appropriate, the adult does not have to keep the mantra going. There will, however, come the day when the child is given a biscuit and they take it without any thanks. The adult then reminds the child by saying something like 'What do we say?' This usually is enough to restore the good behaviour.

With a dog, you are showing them that there are ground rules. With food, you are showing that you have complete control over it, when it is distributed and to whom. In the early days (the first two to three weeks after acquiring your dog) use Priority Feeding. The dog will also be getting information from the other four main behavioural areas and your position will be enhanced with every new signal.

Once the dog has begun to respond to and respect the owner's decisions, it accepts that the 'power of food' is with the owner. Therefore, if the owner decides that today she doesn't want a biscuit before feeding her dog, that's her choice. The rest of the feeding process stays the same – no speech or eye contact, bowl down, move away, dog leaves bowl, bowl removed at once.

The benefit of stopping Priority Feeding after a short time is that you can keep it in reserve. If a little way down the line the dog decides to test a bit or perhaps if the owner has been unwell and is not present at mealtimes for a while, it can be re-introduced for maybe a week. This is in addition to reinforcing the other four areas. This is the canine version of 'What do we say?' The dog will be reminded of the ground rules and should just fall back into place.

If it is necessary to use Enhanced Priority Feeding with a dog it is only used until the dog gets the message. It is then replaced with standard Priority Feeding in the normal way.

Bones

Feeding your dog the correct bones is a very good way of supplying the essential nutrients that enhance your dog's diet. Chewing bones cleans teeth and provides essential and natural nutrients.

Brisket bone is usually the preferred choice among natural diet feeders. It contains a multitude of beneficial food elements that will enrich your dog's diet. We don't use bones as a distracter for bad behaviour or a pacifier, we use them in a meal. They are eaten quickly and therefore offer no opportunity to be guarded and displayed.

There are plenty of books to advise on natural diets and on which types of bones are good for your dog. As Dr Clare Middle confirms, be aware that cooked bones are dangerous because the molecules become set which makes the bones indigestible and causes them to splinter.

Studies in humans have proved that chewing increases blood flow to the brain and aids in reducing anxiety and depression by releasing endorphins. This is no different in any other mammals, especially those that have evolved such huge chewing tools. Let them use these tools appropriately and reap the added benefits.

For a long chew, stag antlers are full of minerals and calcium and the bonus is that they do not splinter. Do remember, though, to remove the antler when it is small enough for a dog to swallow. Cows' hooves are another favourite, although best left for an outside chew as they really do smell dreadful. The great benefit of both is that they are entirely natural.

With chews such as these that tend to last a while, remember to remove them when the dog walks away and offer them on another occasion. As with all food, get the dog to do something to earn its reward, like come to you when called, for example, rather than give out a freebie.

Be aware that a dog chewing and eyeballing you or another dog, rather than relaxing and enjoying the chew, is looking for trouble and sending out a very clear statement: 'This is mine...don't even think about it!' Just walk away from it; don't give it an audience or an excuse to get grumpy. With a dog like this, it would be a great idea to sort out feeding issues and refrain from giving them a treat like this, as it gives them a prime opportunity to display.

- Be aware that some dogs will chew obsessively, which may well indicate anxiety.

- As with anything, give in moderation.

- Remove when the dog has walked away from it, or it may well become a bone of contention, a resource to guard.

- If your dog is possessive over food, then it is not wise to give them a bone that lasts. Something quick and easy – such as brisket bone – is far better and very nourishing.

- Food is a resource and you need to be in charge of it. If dogs take control of food, then a number of issues can arise, resulting not only in aggression but malnutrition, whether due to over- or under-feeding.

It's worth remembering that there's no such thing as a free meal. Don't give dogs food treats for no reason – they must earn them. If, for example, you call it across the room, that's fine. It's been earned, the response has been what you wanted, so be clear that it makes you happy when she comes when called. Recall – the act of calling your dog to you – starts at home in your own domestic setting and garden. If you don't teach it here, you'll have no chance out on your walk.

3

Dealing with Danger

The way we deal with danger is most important, even if we have no idea why the dog is either barking, grumpy or frightened by something. It is not going to help if we chastise it or soothe it either. We need to be proactive and do something sensible that shows the dog in a way it understands that we are in control, and they do not have to worry.

When a dog is threatened, frightened or just plain annoyed, they don't call their solicitors. They growl, bite, cower or run. It's natural, unless you've shown them by your actions that they can trust you to make the correct decisions for them that they can easily understand. Someone has to alert the family to danger and it is invariably your dog, principally as their hearing and sense of smell are far more acute than ours. Do not chastise your dog – welcome the vocal or physical display, but quickly take over and do the right thing.

If you have more than one dog you will find that one dog will bark and the other will back it up; one dog will go in to fight and the other will provide support; one dog will run away and the other will follow. Be the one to make the right decision and guide your dog or dogs to follow you willingly in accepting that decision. Dogs do not suffer fools gladly – you make the wrong decision for your dog and your status as a trustworthy protector will be greatly diminished.

With dogs within a pack, once alerted to a potential threat the decision-makers decide on a course of action that will best ensure they all remain safe. They will base this decision on the three Fs – Flight, Freeze, Fight. There is some debate over the order these options are selected. Most agree that Fight is the last option. From experience, the other two are interchangeable depending on the particular circumstances.

'Flight' does not mean running away in uncontrolled panic. It is used when the decision-maker decides that if things are going to get dangerous here, then the pack should be somewhere safer. The dog will then lead the others to safety in a direction of its choosing. There will be no discussion or dissent from the rest of the pack.

A big difference between us and the free-living canine is that they are not weighed down by possessions. When they leave their original location for a place of safety, they are only leaving ground. Once the danger has passed, they can return and carry on as normal.

'Freeze' relates to a variety of scenarios from 'That's dangerous, but there's no way to move without being noticed. Don't anyone move a muscle...' to 'It's nothing to do with us, don't get involved...' or 'They're not coming our way so they're no threat. Keep an eye on them and alert me to any changes in case I have to change my decision.'

'Fight' is self-explanatory and an option rarely used in the wild. Packs have their own very clearly defined territories and will generally respect those boundaries. They will avoid unnecessary confrontation. In the domestic setting, however, fights among our canines are much more common. We live in close proximity to each other and, unless you are very lucky you won't have a large area of land for the exclusive use of your dog. We get around this by having parks or common land. When you take your dog to the park, it may be confused. Is it his territory, or the Labrador's from next door, or the vicar's Jack Russell, or any of the multitude of other dogs that share this space? Under these circumstances, why wouldn't your dog become confused? One wrong move in terms of body language or eye contact and it's game on. This is why good, ongoing socialisation is so important with the right doggy friends and in the right places.

It must be you that makes that call that leads to the best outcome. Your dog will respect you and your decisions and, in all situations, will look to you for guidance. You must not let it down. And the first place that you will have to make these decisions on a regular basis is at home.

Barking in the Home

When anyone knocks on your front door, they want to speak to someone in the house. In essence, you will have two types of callers: those you will invite into your home; and those you will deal with on the doorstep. You will not know which category you are dealing with until you open that door.

The doorbell rings…potential danger! So your dog barks or indicates to you in some other way. In how many homes when the dog barks at the door is the human response a shouted 'Shut up!' This is a dog we're dealing with here with a limited command of English, so when we respond to being told that danger is approaching the den by shouting, we either tell the dog that we're frightened and that it's the dog's responsibility to make the threat disappear, or that we are barking as well to back it up. Now it feels more confident as it shouts through the door, 'There are two of us here now, so you'd better back off really fast!' It is your responsibility to assess the level of potential danger, not the dog's.

Think back to when you were a little child playing at home with your mother in the back garden hanging the washing out. You see someone coming up your front path. You can't deal with the caller...you're only four...so you call out, 'Mum, there's someone at the door.' It's unlikely that your mother's response would be to shout and tell you to shut up.

Use the same rationale with your dog. It's told you of a potential danger; thank him in a calm, warm voice for doing his job and then deal with the visitor. Say 'Thank you' or any other word of your choosing, but always be consistent. This becomes a very useful sound which the dog comes to recognise in a variety of situations inside and out as 'I'm dealing with it...Everything is under control.'

It is also a good idea not to allow your dog either to greet visitors at the door or accompany you when you see guests off the property. By removing him to a different room or area, you will be reminding him that you are there for him and you don't need support: you can deal with it on your own.

Understand that if the visitor is to be invited in, explain the no speech/eye contact rule to them and ask them to walk straight in and focus on you. Remind them that although your dog is adorable, they have (you hope) come to visit you. Explain to them that they will be able to interact with your dog in a few minutes once it has shown good manners. You will tell your guests when it is OK to call him.

If you are dealing with the visitor at the door, deal with your caller swiftly. Once they have gone, then allow your dog access to the hall so that it can sniff around the front door. It will see you calm and in control after the encounter and you will have shown that you can deal with things without a permanent bodyguard.

This will give you complete control. Your dog will have got into the routine of barking, being thanked and moving without any fuss to another room. You will then be able to manage every situation. If your visitor is frightened of dogs, you will not have to worry about hanging on to your dog while playing 'musical rooms' – you will already be in control, so you can keep your pulse rate down. If you have a child visiting who you do not trust to behave correctly, once again you have no problem. Dog and child do not have to come into contact/conflict. Your pulse rate stays down as a result, and so does your dog's.

You may also like to have your dog on a home line and Happy At Heel harness, which is designed and Patented by PURE Dog Listeners and can be seen in action on www.puredoglisteners.com or on YouTube. It gently guides the dog round to face you, so you can be confident and calm and your dog is guided away effortlessly with no drama, no big deal.

The home line is a line with no loop so it can't get tangled round legs and feet as it trails. You can easily take hold of this when needed again, keeping everything calm and unrushed.

So, if when your dog comes out of the safe room it is really stressed and barking and leapy, then walk it back with no speech, no emotion and no eye contact and stand there with it, blocking his vision from the visitor but hopefully not yours, and you can carry on a calm conversation with them.

When your dog is calm, walk silently out with it round the area before you sit down. This focuses it on you, your calmness and further reduces its anxious state. If it barks, then walk calmly and silently round the room. Your dog may need visual blocking by standing it behind a door with you for support again.

When you enter and the dog is fine after the silent, guided walk round the room, stand on this home line so if the dog decides to launch towards the visitor, you can calmly pick up the home line and guide your dog back to your side, keeping calm and unhurried.

Repeat this as many times as required; the more reactive your dog is, the more times you'll have to do this. Eventually, your dog will relax and this is then the time to let your visitor call it over (unless, of course, you're dealing with cases of aggression). Remember, it can be a lot to ask a dog to go to a visitor for a stroke and cuddle, so if it doesn't go, then that is its prerogative – don't force it to.

Bear in mind that if your visitor gives the dog any cues like eye contact, then the dog will react. Ask your visitor to behave and help you out by not acknowledging there is even a dog in the room. It is hard, but necessary.

Your dog, your rules, your house. Be strong.

Beware the self-styled 'dog expert' guest who does not follow instructions – the type who goes straight into a dog's personal space despite all the signals the dog is giving and then is surprised when the dog bites. If a guest refuses to help you resolve your problems, it's better you keep human and dog apart. If a visitor to a house with children was asked not to give the children sweets because they were undergoing dental treatment, very few people would hand over a big bag of sweets to them saying, 'Don't take any notice of what your mum and dad say, eat up.' Yet people don't think twice about interfering with dogs against the owner's wishes. It's often the case that the person who ignores your request will be the first to complain when the dog bites them.

Barking in the Garden

If the dogs are in the garden and bark at something, even if you have no idea why they are barking (they can smell and hear so much better than us), remember to acknowledge this using 'Thank you' or 'Carrots' or anything in an assertive but friendly manner...as long as you are consistent with the word and tone. As before, this is your trigger word for you taking over the situation and making decisions over the best plan of action whenever your dog is anxious.

In the garden, thank your dog, and walk away with it to another area, blocking its view. Then release the dog when it is calm.

With some dogs, you'll have to go back into the house initially, even further from the trigger, to calm them. Walking away from things that dogs find fearful is the natural thing to do. It is the same for us. We may not think our neighbours are an issue, but our dog doesn't know that. You have to show your dog in a way that it understands. Listen to your dog's concerns and act on them. It is not being mischievous for the sake of it, just frightened or concerned about what may happen, so do something positive to reassure it. Remember, if you stroke it and say 'There, there, then…' you are praising it and rewarding it for feeling stressed. Do as instructed above and you'll get through to your dog loud and clear.

Barking out on a Walk

You, the ultimate decision-maker, must be the one to decide whether to use Freeze, Flight or Fight. If you see or hear something ahead that you don't like or you think might frighten or annoy your dog, just deviate from your intended route without any drama and it will come with you. Problem solved, before it becomes a problem.

If your dog notices something before you (it may be a sound or smell that you haven't yet sensed), say 'Thank you' as soon as you pick up on the often subtle indications, and move away as you would do at home. Using the consistent trigger word and tone will tell your dog, 'I'm taking control of the situation now, no problem.'

This may just mean crossing the road to avoid confrontation, stepping back into a driveway because of skateboarders on the pavement or may involve no action at all. You will be saying to your dog,

'Thanks for that, but I've already got it in hand.' If your dog indicates that it's frightened by cowering or lunging, do not force them to confront their fears – simply walk away.

As you progress with this deviation regime, you'll find that as time goes on you'll be deviating far less and your dog will be looking to you for a decision when anxious. So don't walk about with your mobile phone in hand and ignoring your dog's indications on the other end of the lead. You're supposed be going for a walk together, so interact and enjoy your dog's company, and it will enjoy yours. By being fun, it'll be focused on you and not left to ponder what may happen. If you're really enjoying your walk, then all must be well.

Checklist for Dealing with Danger

- When a visitor arrives, your dog may bark or indicate by just looking out of the window or walking to the door. It's doing a great job, but now this is your signal to take over.

- Acknowledge your dog with a word in an assertive but friendly manner. You can say anything – 'Thank you', 'Bananas', it doesn't matter – as long as you always use the same word. Call your dog to you.

- Take your dog in a calm, positive way to an alternative room, e.g. the kitchen (you are placing it away from the arrival of visitors, and making it your job to deal with them).

- If your dog is very upset and still barking madly when your visitor enters, ask the visitor to sit in another room.

- Go to the room your dog is in. Hold the dog on a lead until it is quiet and then walk to where your visitor is, you leading your dog, not the other way round.

- If your dog is quiet, great. Say nothing, don't make a fuss of it. If it's quiet and gentle, you both stay.

- If it gets too excited with visitors, guide it away.

- If it sniffs and is gentle, then let it.

- If the dog leaps/bounds/barks, hold it on a home line and calmly walk it round with no speech, no eye contact and no emotion, while you chat to your visitors. If it is still upset, then block its view by walking it behind a wall. When it has calmed, walk out with it.

- If you know your dog's going to become stressed in advance, then have it on a home line in preparation, so it doesn't make contact with a visitor who may also get it wrong. It keeps you calm and in control, too.

- In the garden or at windows, thank your dog, call it to you and take it to another area and calmly hold or simply shut the door to the area of concern. You saw what was happening, you determined there was no threat, and you are getting on with your life. No big deal.

- If on a walk and your dog pulls after something, then take the option of flight – walk away calmly and reward and praise at heel. Simply change your direction, even before your dog lunges. Make the right decision for it before it can react. Your dog will be impressed!

4

Aggression

There are very few naturally aggressive dogs: it is normally their environment and experiences that make then so. Aggressive behaviour does not just happen out of the blue; the signals can sometimes build gradually over many months, and when the dog feels it has just had enough, it erupts. And you should always remember that a dog bite can cause serious injury, from bruising right through to lacerations, scarring and, in serious cases, broken bones and even fatalities.

And don't be lulled into a false sense of security. Any dog, whatever their size or breed, if wrongly brought up, can turn from a sweet, cuddly little angel into a snarling devil.

Aggression that causes damage and bloodshed in harmonious canine or wolf packs and families in the wild is very rare indeed. Aggression will only be shown towards an unwelcome visitor to ensure safety and survival.

Aggression in dogs is fairly common nowadays – indeed, research shows that 50 per cent of all dogs will have an aggressive encounter of one form or another. We have so many more dogs on our streets, and many of them think that they have to protect themselves and their family with the only weapons they have – their teeth. It's perfectly natural if you think about it – if you are not family, you are not welcome.

In our world with our domestic dog, it is so important to teach them self-control and boundaries of behaviour. They need to be treated like dogs – not humans – or you end up with a whole host of issues, the most disturbing being aggression.

Any breed and any personality can become aggressive, and ultimately it is because we make it happen, either from poor socialisation, dog-on-dog interactions or bad experiences with humans. Dogs can become aggressive towards anything through fear, by being made to confront their nemesis head on. They can fear losing what they want and need, and fear for their safety.

As with children, you get what you're given as far as personality is concerned, but you nurture and bring them up as positively as possible – if unacceptable behaviour is shown, then you can help modify the behaviour so they can be accepted wherever they go.

So be aware that:

- If a dog is being teased, or you are being confrontational by staring directly into its eyes, it will be fearful and react.

- There is the danger of an aggressive response if a dog is pounced on from a deep sleep. 'Let sleeping dogs lie...' is commonly said for a very good reason. If you want to cuddle a dog, call it into your space. It will not feel threatened, it has not initiated your movement and so will not be given the opportunity to tell you off either. The dog comes to you and if it feels uneasy about the encounter for any reason, then it can decide not to join you.

- Never kiss or put your face close to a strange dog, even if
  you know its owner well. The dog doesn't really know you.
  It will be seen as a confrontation, an attack. People are often
  seen fawning over dogs that are not theirs despite obvious
  signals that the dog isn't happy. Many potential victims are
  lucky that a lot of dogs put up with a huge amount of strange,
  insensitive human behaviour.

Dealing with Aggression

Dogs are fearful of potential threats, whether *we* think they are a
threat or not. It is up to the owner to respond in the correct manner
to show the dog that its fears are unfounded and there is no issue.
Shouting 'Shut up' at a dog only adds fuel to the fire.

Who decides what is a 'danger'? If we get it wrong, then the dog
decides. You have to trade places with your dog and show it that *you* will
make the right decisions when appropriate, not the other way round.

Some owners say, 'But my dog growls at me…not other people.'
This is just your dog putting you in your place – the caring family
member, just giving you a ticking off. 'If you do that, you'll get hurt…'
or 'Don't sit there, that's my place…' or 'Who are you to tell me what
to do?' or 'Get away from my food.' It's exactly the same attitude as
you telling your child not to do something. But dogs can't talk – they
only show their thoughts and feelings physically and vocally.

We have to show them, 'You can't push me around, mate!' The
way we do this is in a gentle and considerate way, with kindness and
empathy. Don't get into a fight with your dog because you will come
off far worse than he or she will – you can't demand submission; you
have to act like the adult and, above all, keep safe.

It's never advisable to make your dog submit by forcing it on its
side and holding it down – you could well be setting yourself up for
a disaster. Give it the right information so that it naturally submits to

you, because of the way you are and not because you have resorted to force.

If you have been advised to opt for castration to help control aggressive behaviour, look p.156 and research the options more carefully. The cause is often in the head, not the tackle!

Aggression towards People

Some dogs are aggressive just to men, some just to women or some just to children – and some are aggressive to all. And if a dog becomes over-protective of you, then it will be aggressive to anyone who comes near you.

Professional help should always be sought when trying to correct this behaviour. It would be foolhardy here to give guidance in correction as we have to take each individual case on its merits and act accordingly. This is naturally true of all other behavioural issues, but getting this aspect of behaviour correction wrong could have very serious consequences. Methods of correction will vary depending on the dog's personality, the owner's personality and capabilities. Keep you and others safe and be sure to get a vet's opinion before any behavioural work is undertaken.

Food Aggression

To ensure their dog never becomes aggressive over food, many dog owners have been taught to take the bowl away while it is feeding. Well, any chocolate lover would tell you that if you gave them a chocolate bar and then decided to take it from them halfway through, you'd have a fight on your hands. They might even become irritated…then angry…then aggressive. 'You gave it to me and now you want it back? Can't make your mind up?' Depending on your personality, you may do one of two things: (1) give it to me for a quiet life; or (2) fight me for it.

Don't set yourself up for a failure. If you give, then do just that – give. Keep it clear and straightforward, and avoid confusing signals. Don't tease a dog with anything and particularly not with food. You are messing with survival instincts if you do. Also, do read the section on Enhanced Priority Feeding again (p. 33) which will help to reinforce some key points.

On-lead Aggression

Your dog may be great off the lead running around the park, playing with other dogs and people. But when on the lead, some people find that their dog is aggressive to other dogs (and other things).

From the dog's perspective, when it is off-lead it is free to run away whenever it feels things are not quite right or feels threatened. If that dog is on the lead then it has lost the option of Flight – it is tethered and cannot flee. The only options left to it are Freeze or Fight. It can't get away, so the only true option that is left is to get in there, show aggression and prepare for Fight. Some dogs are all mouth and no action, and may spend much of their time just barking ferociously. This is still a dog making decisions, saying, 'Stay out of my space or else.' Even if that dog has always previously backed off, one day he may feel like he has no option but to bite.

If your dog trusts you to make the right decision, when he sees danger then he will be happy by your side for *you* either to take the Flight, Freeze or Fight option. We won't ever choose the Fight option, but will always select the option that will make your dog feel safe in your hands and then choose to follow your lead:

- If you take flight before your dog even reacts, you are simply changing the direction of your walk.

- If you take flight when it is thinking about being concerned, you're taking its mind off the object of focus and on to you and showing it that you're not in the least concerned.

- If your dog has reacted with barking and lunging and you then turn, you are showing it that there is no need for that – evasive action and keeping safe is better – and always praise and reward at heel. Sorted! Job done!

Dogs are reactive when stressed or in a position of authority. We have the capacity to be proactive, and show them we are calm and great at decisions when all seems rather uncertain in their world.

Walk away, and your dog has to follow – it's on a lead – and say nothing, other than an assertive 'Come on' or 'Thank you'. Don't tug the lead, as it will become the trigger of the dog's focus, and you'll be seen as an instigator of the fight, an anxious follower. Be that strong, silent type that avoids confrontation. Praise your dog when he is back at heel, and your dog will thank you for making a great decision.

In the (p. 67) chapter Walking Your Dog, the use of stooges is discussed in detail, and you could make use of this tactic when looking to avoid confrontation. No dog truly wants to fight – give it the chance to walk away and it will be happy.

Inter-pack Aggression

I often get calls from owners whose dogs are fighting among themselves. This generally happens when the owners enter the room and not when the dogs are left alone together. If this only happens when the owners are present, it is an indication of hierarchy 'discussions' and a debate about who's looking after the pack/family when they are all together. Both dogs think they are the one capable of the job and literally fight for it. Now, if the job of leader was taken by the human, then these discussions would not be necessary.

Another variation on this scenario is if there is what I would refer to as 'a bully in the pack', and the attacks will seem unprovoked. It may be just a growl, a look, a nip or a full-on attack – intimidation is being used to keep all the others in their place. The aggression may be apparent at feeding time, or walking through narrow doorways, when one has possession of a toy, when non-household members enter the house or on a walk when they are both attached to a lead and something ahead is clearly a concern.

Also, sometimes one dog resting in bed or under a table will growl at another as it passes. The meaning is clear: 'My space! Don't come close unless invited. I'm boss.'

Can you see a pattern here? The five components (p. 24) run as a common theme throughout this book, and are very apparent: they are triggered during times of danger, feeding, trophy possession, who goes through the door first and who is decision-maker when the pack rejoins.

How to Avoid Being Bitten

If you are out and about, do not go up to stroke every dog you see. Always ask the owner and respect their wishes. If they say no, it doesn't automatically mean the dog is a biter, it may just be shy and anxious.

When you enter a dog's space, you may be perceived as a threat. Of course, most dogs are perfectly friendly and the only danger you will face is being coated in hair and saliva. But if the dog is unsure of you and your intentions, it will react with one of the three Fs outlined in the chapter on Dealing with Danger: Flight, Freeze or Fight. (p. 39)

In Flight mode, if a dog can get away even to the bottom of the garden or into another room, it will be happy. Under no circumstances approach it or attempt to placate it. If you restrict its ability to flee, it may have to resort to Fight.

In Freeze, if a dog doesn't want to interact – because it's either fearful or shy – it may choose to stay very still and turn its head away, in an effort to calm the situation down. If it is on a lead, it only has this option, followed by the next – the bite. Usually if you ignore the dog it will be happy to return the favour. It may first run away then stop and assess the situation, before fleeing further or relaxing, accepting there is no threat.

A dog will react in Fight mode if the first two methods have failed or it is fearful while stuck on the end of a lead or protecting its territory. Most aggression is born of fear. There are very few naturally aggressive dogs.

Checklist for Avoiding Being Bitten

- Do not approach dogs that are not yours. Ask the owner if you can call them over for a stroke, do not stare dogs in the eye and do not wave your arms around or run away. Treat them with respect by respecting their personal space.

- If you need to visit an address where you have reason to believe a dog is running free, assess the situation before you enter. If you are worried, stay on the public side of the door/ gate. Make contact with the occupants by calling out or by using your mobile phone. Ask them either to secure the dog or come out and deal with you at the gate.

- If you do enter the property and are then approached by a dog, stand still, arms by your sides, not speaking and using no eye contact. Once you have been checked out and feel it's safe to move, do, but do it smoothly and calmly. Walk confidently – you are not a threat.

- If once inside you are unhappy about the situation, back slowly away still sticking rigidly to the no eye contact and no speech rule.

- Remember, it takes no more time to think than it does to panic.

- Ideally, the owner should already have or be able to take control of the dog, but not everyone realises that the world may not adore their dog in the way they do. They may also be blissfully unaware of the potential impact if their dog becomes aggressive. How often have we heard, 'It's all right...he's only playing.' Oh, so that's all right then? Even after their dog has bitten, some owners remain unperturbed. Their two favourite phrases are: 'It's only a nip...' or 'It's your fault...you must have upset him.' As you can see, you cannot always rely on the owner to do the right thing, so you need to look to your own safety in such cases.

- If it becomes probable that you are about to be bitten, try to give the dog a target – they will generally bite anything thrust at them so a clipboard, briefcase or anything the dog can target rather than you is good. If they can pull it from you then that item becomes a trophy and they will often run around with their prize, allowing you to make your exit.

- If the worst happens, try to keep on your feet. If knocked to the ground, curl into a ball with your hands over your ears and remain motionless. Try not to scream or roll around.

- To avoid making a difficult situation worse, **do not**:
  - Shout at a dog.
  - Show any aggression.
  - Scream and/or run.
  - Put yourself between owner and dog.
  - Invade the dog's personal space.
  - Go too near a bitch with a litter.

Most importantly, *never* ignore any signals that the dog is giving you. Most dogs don't want to bite you, but if they feel they have to, then they will. Dogs are not Walt Disney characters; a dog only knows how to be a dog. If we understand that and respect the dog, we will usually have a safe resolution.

5

Keeping Calm

The Calm Hold

Can you think clearly and logically when in a state of panic? Of course not. To make progress, we always need to start and finish with a calm, thinking dog and human.

To deal with any nervous reaction, obsessive behaviour or to just give a dog time to think and moderate its behaviour, use the 'Calm Hold':

- Take the dog by the collar and draw it to your side and place the palm of your hand on its shoulders gently. Calm – Palm – No speech. And no eye contact, no emotion.

- At first the dog will probably continue to shake, attempt to chase its tail, or perform some other undesirable behaviour.

- As the dog realises that you are relaxed and your pulse rate low, it will ask itself the question: 'Why am I doing this?'

- The dog will then gradually relax and you will be able to release it, again with no speech or eye contact. Be prepared to repeat if required.

- If your dog struggles with this, then do not hold for too long. Give it the opportunity to wander round some more, then, as it passes, you try again.

- Having a home line on will help you guide your dog back to you with no fuss.

This works particularly well with tail chasers, humping dogs and panting, stressed dogs who are leaning into you for support on firework night. If you lean back, you're there for them; if you soothe them with strokes and kind voices, you're more likely to exacerbate the issue.

Each time you use the Calm Hold, the time taken for the dog to relax will decrease. It takes as long as it takes. Every dog is an individual. When dealing with a problem that will last for a while, such as on Bonfire Night, it is useful to have a pile of magazines to hand and to sit on the floor looking through them. This makes it more comfortable for you if you have to hold the dog for long periods. Some dogs will take to the Calm Hold better if you use your legs. In this instance, if it is trembling at your feet or on the sofa, simply place your legs over the dog gently. The dog will feel your calmness and follow suit.

It is also a benefit to have soft classical music playing in the background. This has been proven to calm your dog and it certainly calms me. I also like lavender wafting in the air. It all helps, but don't forget it's what *you* do that is so important as well. A snug-fitting coat helps in these situations, too, but don't just rely on add-ons.

The Calm Hold is not a great idea for those dogs who are not keen on close contact, are hand shy or who haven't had much human contact before. In these cases, it is great to use the Calm Walk; this is also a great addition out and about or just settling a dog when people have arrived and it's being rather reactive.

The Calm Walk

This is a great method for outside *and* inside, because when you put a stressed dog into a Calm Hold, you are telling it to stop, and it may think that freezing is a strange idea when it seems as though the best option would be to flee. So the simple steps to achieve a Calm Walk are:

- With no emotion, speech or eye contact, walk your dog round, which puts its focus back on to you and off the distraction. You're showing it that you lead and the dog will follow. 'Trust me...look to me...I'm here for you.'

- It is also helpful to begin with to block the dog's view after walking away, using a tree or car, for example, so the distraction becomes invisible. Calm Hold there, which is probably easier by just putting slight tension on the lead rather than your hand on his neck.

- Do not just block the view with your body as another dog walks past. Your dog will most likely react and will then wonder what on earth you are trying to achieve by putting yourself in the line of fire.

As in the Dealing with Danger chapter (p. 39), you need to show your dog that you can be trusted to take the right action when needed, even if you have no idea why your dog is stressed out. Do right by your dog and it will learn to trust you through thick and thin.

By following these simple steps, your dog won't need to be aggressive or shrink into a corner or hug the fence as you walk along the road. It can look to you with your calm, assertive and happy manner and gain strength from you.

It'll be happy in the knowledge that it doesn't have to worry about a thing, just have fun. He'll relax both in and out of the home. Very reactive dogs can take time to change their minds, but be persistent and remember to include all five elements.

6

Walking Your Dog

The walk is an important part in a dog's day, a time you should enjoy together. It should be fun. The walk encompasses: (1) lead walking – ideally a gentle stroll with you as a relaxed, smiling leader, with your dog looking to you for guidance; (2) off-lead – your dog should be a master at coming back when called. This is where having a 'stop button' request is essential. Off-lead also incorporates play; we forget as dogs grow up that they are play machines, something that is dealt with in the chapter Bonding Through Play (p. 88).

It does not matter where the walk takes place. It is who you are with, not where you are, that is all important. So don't put you or your dog in a situation too soon that neither of you is able to cope with.

In order to understand how we get great walks on- and off-lead, it is worth understanding why dogs pull on leads and why they won't respond to you off-lead. Dogs don't ask other dogs either to heel or come back. They follow each other in groups and look out for which direction the leader takes them. If they lose the pack, they are vulnerable. So this is a form of control only exerted by humans, but necessary in our world.

Our approach is to revert to nature and get the dog to follow you because it wants to and not because you have made it. And get it to come when called because you have decided to change the route, or do something else, and you are fun and worth coming back to.

Why Do Dogs Pull?

Because:

- We let them.

- They are impatient to get to the destination.

- We follow the tug.

- We possibly gave up trying to get them to heel as youngsters.

- They are on the lookout for their nemesis which they have to face en route.

- They are more interested in everything and everyone else than you and are completely disregarding of owner.

- Dogs pull toward anything to investigate.

- They want to lunge or bark at their nemesis.

- Dogs can be more aggressive on the lead than off. Why? Because off-lead they can communicate as they wish, they can meet as they wish and make the right decision for them and are not forced into what they see as a confrontation. They haven't got a human on the other end of a lead making incorrect decisions or fuelling nervous/aggressive behaviour.

- Approaching humans may also be focusing on your dogs and trying to get eye contact which can seem confrontational to a dog. So veer away at 90 degrees to break that eye contact. As humans, we feel uncomfortable if a stranger locks eye contact with us. A dog will feel just as threatened and it is merely a small step from conflict.

Calm everything down and get them into a thinking state of mind.

The Walk (Follow Me)

The Happy At Heel Harness designed by PURE Dog Listeners is a side attachment harness that quickly helps you teach your dog to walk with you and look to you. Its design ensures you can easily turn your dog towards you with little effort.

You can make teaching walking to heel into a game of 'Follow Me'; have fun with it and your dog will enjoy it, too. Don't walk around like a sergeant major demanding attention; get good heel work by being fun and interesting, not demanding and boring. Ultimately, you will want your dog to walk by your side, but the first part of the game is to get it to focus and follow you.

Work on this at home inside or outside. Walk backwards so you are face to face, sideways, have a squeaky toy, get your dog to want to be there. Look at your dog, not at your destination, and engage with it. Make this happen off-lead at home initially, so you are not relying on the physical tool and can concentrate on how engaging you are.

Home and close to home is a great learning environment where there are fewer distractions and triggers. This helps to focus your dog on you and also focuses you on what you're doing and stops you relying on the lead, which should ultimately be there as a final resort. Again, it is who you are with, not where you are, that is important. We're saying, 'We know what's important to you and we'll show you that you can trust us. Then we'll show you a world where you can just live life to the full.'

Before you start the walking out and about, it is vital that you and your dog are relaxed – this means that you and your dog will be in a thinking frame of mind and learning will be possible.

You may well have to desensitise your dog to all the triggers that make it over-react prior to the walk. We want your dog to look excited but with some self-control. Both human and canine must be in a calm state before the walk begins. So get into the habit of having the lead out and about – just because the lead is in view it doesn't mean you're off on a walk. You may want to clean it or put it around your neck as the next fashion accessory! If your dog gets over-excited when you put your wellies on, for example, then put them on and have a cuppa, and when the dog is calm then call your dog over and put the lead on and start your walk. Remember, dogs learn by what we do, so don't necessarily follow action A with action B until they are calm. You're not being cruel, you're doing things in your own time.

Lots of short practice walks in a day are better than doing one long one and getting it wrong. Your short ones gradually become longer as the days go by and, before you know it, you'll be off around the countryside having a lovely time together. When I mean short, to begin with you'll be doing probably ten minutes, five or six times a day. As the time increases, then the number of times decrease. This means short-term pain for you in exchange for a long-term gain for all. If your dog becomes agitated because you have changed your routine and displays the attitude of 'We go out now!' please remember it is because you have now changed your routine for good reason – *you* make the decision over where and when you go out.

Yes, dogs do need exercise and you *will* enjoy your long walks again, but it's best to leave these for when everything's working well, and you are both happy, confident and safe.

It's also worth thinking about playing some of the many team-building games in the house and garden to enhance your bond. Your dog will love them and get the physical exercise and education it needs, too.

If you can resist the temptation to take your dog out into the big wide world before it is ready, and convince it to really believe that you can be trusted to make all the right decisions, then you will reap the benefits. However, we know that all sorts of pressures can be brought to bear on you. It's common to hear, 'You must walk your dog for an hour in the morning and again at night.' If you must, then remember not to let your dog take the lead, with you ending up in the tug of war. Stop, turn and go where you want to.

I can also appreciate that we live in the real world and that not everybody has a garden. In such cases, of course, you have to take your dog outside if only for toileting purposes. If you fall into this category, then it is even more important that you consistently give your dog the right signals and that you have a plan as to what you will do if the situation changes. If you stand hopping from one foot to another not knowing what to do, your dog's reaction will be 'Lead, follow or get out of the way'. Uncertainty is the first sign of panic.

Who leads the walk, decides where to go and how long it lasts? You do. Therefore, when you leave the house, all humans should go through the front door first, at their speed. If the dog respects you, it will be alongside you or follow you. Do not force a sit; we want it naturally to look to you and wait to see what you are going to do and which way you will go, not launch itself out of the door with no regard for your authority.

So, with lead on, you should walk to and from the front door. When the dog is calm, open up the door. If the dog barges through, simply stop, turn back into the house and try again... and again... until your dog gets it right. Take a break if this seems to exacerbate the situation, and try again later. If you do this with no speech or eye contact, just praise when the dog gets it right, you'll get the job done. And the praise should be quiet and gentle, or you might just flick that excitable switch back on again. Try going out a different door if you have one. Remember, don't be predictable as that is what your dog is responding to.

Your dog should be on a lead even if you are only going to your car. If you are going to drive, then when you get to your destination it should only come out of the car on the lead even if you are on the common. Walk a short distance from the car (ten or fifteen metres is fine) before you release it. This reminds the dog that you are the decision-maker, not him, and that today you have decided that the walk will start from...here.

If you are not happy letting your dog off the lead, then have it on a nine-metre line attached to the Happy At Heel Harness and refer to the 'Teaching the Recall' section on page 97. Safety first – you only have to be unlucky once.

During the walk, call your dog back to you at irregular intervals. Place him on a lead, try a small amount of heel work or just walk on the lead for twenty metres or so with him, then make a big fuss of him and release him again. This will make training both fun and teach your dog that being put on a lead does not always mean the end of the walk. Keep the walk interesting. Don't always take the same route, alter your pace, turn left, turn right, stop, walk backwards. Keep the dog guessing, 'Where are we going now? What are we going to do?' Don't forget to turn a different way occasionally on leaving home just to keep your dog wondering. Even walking the usual route but on the opposite pavement to normal will keep your dog on its toes.

Aggression Towards Other Dogs

Get your walk right first in areas where there are no dogs – at home, car parks etc. Then when these are going well, you can move on to the next stage.

Let's take the uncertainty and embarrassment away. Consider the use of 'stooges' – make enquiries of your friends and acquaintances to find people who have dogs and would be prepared to help you. The two things you might worry about most are meeting another dog (so let's make that happen in controlled conditions) and the disapproval of the other dog owner. If they are working with you, then that won't happen. Remember, though, even before your one-to-one work with your dog and stooge, do make sure your dog is focused on you when you are around people without dogs. Do the easy stuff first.

Arrange to meet your stooge in a dog-free zone if possible, so you know they're the only ones you have to prepare for. Even if your dog barks or shows aggression to the other dog, just thank it and walk behind your car or another obstacle to block its view and continue with the Calm Walk (p. 59). If you are doing this outside your home, you can simply walk back inside.

When your dog is calm, you can walk into view again, making sure that the stooge pairing are at least fifty metres away and facing in another direction. Make this a short lesson and leave on a good note; don't push for a perfect dog first time out. It will take time for you to master the assertive 'Thank you' as you've done in the home, and do the rest with no eye contact and no emotion to bring your dog back to a calm state.

Each time you turn away from the danger and walk towards home or your car, the more confident your dog will become in your decisions until you get to a stage where your dog trusts you simply to walk past on the other side of the road something that used to be an issue.

If there was a potential threat ahead that bothered your child or granny, then crossing the road or walking away would be a natural thing for you to do. You are not showing them you're a coward, you're showing them that you will take care of them – that this decision is the right one to take right now.

It is a great idea to pre-empt your dog's reaction and take evasive action even before your dog has reacted. As has been noted already, you can be proactive where your dog is only reactive in situations it is unsure of. If you can make an assertive decision, then your dog will become confident in your ability to take the right action in times of doubt.

Other Dogs Off-lead

Have you ever been in a situation where a loose dog has been racing towards you and you haven't had a clue what to do? Try this – it works more often than not. Call your dog to you and walk away at right angles. You are showing the invader you are neither going to be scared away nor a threat. Giving the side-on view is one of disinterest in joining in and non-confrontational. Walk round in an arc if the dog follows you, and politely ask the owner to put their dog on a lead until you are out of sight.

Eye Contact

We use eye contact, or the lack of it, to show a huge variety of emotions. As was mentioned earlier, canines do not make eye contact with one another until they want to interact, and then it will not be prolonged eye contact, unless for the purposes of a heated discussion or play. Dogs greet by sniffing the undercarriage and ears, and show respect by giving no prolonged eye contact to establish 'Who are you?' and 'Nice to meet you.' It is a polite exchange. Well-mannered and thinking relaxed dogs will turn their heads briefly as they pass each other on a path or ignore the other completely. However, a dog in a heightened state will be giving all the wrong signals and this is where the lunging and panic sets in.

Many adult dogs will not tolerate young bouncy adolescence. Can you blame them? Good manners come with practice, which is why teaching boundaries and ongoing good socialisation is so important in the first two years of life and beyond.

So when you are walking along a road or path with your dog and another dog is coming head on to you, frothing and straining on the lead, just move away 90 degrees. Try to understand that although you don't see it as an issue, your dog probably will. It puts dogs in an awkward position, and add to this that we are holding them by the lead, making them face each other. Your dog will focus on the other dog, and not the competence or otherwise of the owner.

You will find many dogs are great off-lead, but not on-lead, as they are able to greet each other in a way that is natural to them. So help your dog out, and walk on the other side of the road as you pass any dog. And if you want to meet, make sure they are not eye to eye but given the space to greet naturally. They will then give eye contact when they are ready. When that interaction is complete, eye contact is broken. This is similar to us in many ways.

Play and challenge are two of the main reasons that dogs make prolonged eye contact. How to tell the difference? Body language, pure and simple.

A dog making a challenge will be standing very still with hard eye contact towards the other dog. It will be fully engaged and making itself look as big as possible – tail up and drawn up to its full height. Its body will be tense, like a coiled spring, just waiting for the release given by the response of the other dog, which will be either to meet the challenge by maintaining eye contact, or indicate with lowered tail and averted eyes that it is not 'up for it'. The dog unwilling to take up the challenge will not move (except to turn its head to avert its eyes), until the aggressor indicates it is willing to 'let it go'.

To move before this occurs would not be wise. If your dog is averting its eyes like this, it is motionless for a very good reason. If you want to call it, make sure you do it at a 90-degree angle away from the other dog. This move will be neither a challenge nor a flee indication to the aggressor, so the aggressor is less likely to react. Let dogs speak dog to each other; it is we who cause problems for them.

Prolonged eye contact as an invitation to play is quite different. Soft, bright eyes, the play bow, wagging tail, and very often the open-mouthed, tongue-lolling grin – everything indicating a non-threatening desire to play. This may be matched by the other dog and, if it is, then 'game on'. Interestingly, if the other dog does not want to play, the signals it returns vary very little from the dog not wishing to engage in a fight – averted eyes, head turned away. Often it will just walk away, something it would not dare to do in the other scenario until the aggressor accepts its reluctance to fight and breaks off the contact.

Checklist for Walking Your Dog

- *You* decide who leads the walk, where to go and how long for. This is a game of 'Follow Me', *not* tug of war!

- Start off-lead in the home – there are fewer distractions here so it should be more straightforward. When this is working, progress to a garden or quiet, outside space. There is no time limit on getting it right. Be patient.

- Look at your dog – you are interacting with it, so when it glances up the immediate reward is your kind and happy face. Walk backwards, have a toy with you, make yourself interesting.

- If your dog jumps up, stop – no eye contact, no speech, no emotion. If this happens later while on a lead, hold the lead out at arm's length so the dog does not get contact with you. When the dog calms, continue.

- Short and sweet lessons. If your dog loses focus, call it back, have another go. It's not your dog's fault; it may feel stressed and need a break. Finish on a good note.

- Move to on-lead in house and garden, taking it slow, and still within the boundary of your home. Do this at least four times a day, building on time gradually as you and your dog get better. Go at your dog's learning speed.

- When at heel, give reward and praise regularly. If the dog goes in front, stop, rest, then walk in another direction. Reward and praise when back at heel. You may have to walk backwards initially to keep great eye contact.

- Test your dog out – stop every now and again. If your dog is tuned in to you, it will stop as well, so praise it. If, however, it carries on, let it. It will stop when it gets to the end of the lead. Then call your dog to you and begin again.

- Testing the stop is as important as walking.

- Try just moving one foot forward and stop. Just because you've done A doesn't mean B is going to happen; this will focus your dog on you.

- Progress further outside the boundary as the elements of the walk fall into place.

- Short and sweet is a good rule of thumb – too long and you'll get it wrong.

- Have fun, be fun and *animated* with a quiet dog; try being cooler and more calm using long vowel sounds for a reactive dog to get its attention.

- With a bouncy dog, you will have to be quieter but still interesting.

- Do not go the same way every time; do not be predictable.

- Be relaxed at every stage; if you lose your dog's focus, go back to where you had it and begin again.

- Be prepared to call a walk off if you are not getting this feeling after five to ten minutes.

- If you have a dog that runs off and doesn't come back, do not let it off the lead until you have a completely relaxed and focused dog wherever you go on-lead. Use short or long line.

- When you do let off a short lead, have a long line to make you feel more confident. If the dog does not recall immediately, you can reel it in. Do short line work for a couple of minutes, then have another go.

- You can play 'Follow Me' on the long line. Just walk off at 90 degrees and if your dog is attentive it will turn and move in your direction.

- Be inviting and fun when your dog comes to you.

- Remember, a walk does not have to mean a forced march. Play en route, give time for standing and staring at your surroundings and sniffy time for your dog.

- All this takes time and patience – and some dogs require more than others of both.

- Again, it's worth repeating that it doesn't matter *where* you are – it is *who you are with* that is important.

- The way we teach and learn is all in the dog's time. Be patient with your dog and get it to follow you with a happy gait and a gentle wag. Walking with your dog on a lead should be a pleasure and a chance to bond and get to know each other. It's another valuable opportunity to get a connection.

7

Rejoining and Affection

Dogs who know each other, live together and who think clearly, greet each other in a gentle manner, not bossing or bullying each other or in a way that could be misconstrued by either to be aggressive or rude. Pups greeting a parent will lick the parent's lips to encourage regurgitation; it is a passive reaction you will see in adult dogs, too. Presenting belly up is passive as well, possibly too passive. If a dog does this immediately on your arrival, it is generally in dog terms a way to defuse a situation it is unsure about. Some may urinate as you bend down to stroke them, so don't do it; wait for the dog to walk away, then when you are ready, get close to the floor and call the dog into your space, being careful not to lean over it. Don't crowd a dog or loom over it, as this is intimidating. Remember, you are very tall to a dog, and a stranger can be very scary.

How our dogs approach us on rejoining after a separation is very telling of how they perceive us. Yes, we are happy to see them and they are happy to see us. But we need some politeness as well. We do not either wish to be mugged or licked to death while squeezing through a door with children, bags or granny. We could do with respect on both sides; personal space is precious and a hooligan putting paw graffiti all over our clothing is unwelcome.

Now if a dog stands back when you enter and is not bounding into your space, then why not call it to you for a quick hello and a stroke. If, on the other hand, your welcome is not calm and gentle, then we have to be rather more strict and set some ground rules.

There is the dog that will stay in its bed and always expect you to go over and pay homage to it. The dog is now prompting your movement; it can tell you off at any moment and call a halt to your affections. Do not go to your dog – call it to you. It has to respect your decisions and that you'd like a cuddle or interaction now, so ask it to come into your space, then when you are ready you may finish the interaction, all neat, tidy and safe – all on your terms. Movement is powerful; you create your dog's movement, not the other way round.

It is the same when a dog leaps on to your lap for a cuddle uninvited. You are now leading it to believe that it has the right to end the interaction – 'I've started so I'll finish!' So do not put yourself in this potentially awkward situation. It is for you to start and finish in your time, not your dog's.

· When using the following techniques, you won't be either rude or cruel; quite the opposite, you will be showing that you are strong, trustworthy and caring. And none of these techniques require you to act like a drill sergeant.

Rejoining takes place many times a day with us and our dogs. Whenever you leave your dog for any reason they will, on your return, go through various rituals of greetings depending who has entered. If they are mugging you and attempting to gain attention in an unruly manner, it is vital that you give them no cues, either verbally or by eye or physical contact. If they jump up in your face or try to climb on to your lap for attention, just firmly guide them away, again with no cues of any kind. It is best to have a collar on your dog (if it has no neck issues) so you can do this effectively without having to grab skin, which will be seen as an aggressive and intimidating type of contact by your dog. Leave the dog for a few moments after it has settled before you call it.

When *you* are ready, call your dog to you for a fuss. Use its name gently along with the request – 'Here'… 'Come'… 'Potatoes'… it doesn't matter what word you use, just make sure it is always the same one, as it is only a sound to them. Elongate your vowels to make your voice softer and, when your dog does come to you, continue with the long vowels to keep your dog calm. Don't be inclined then to make a fuss of your dog in an over-excited way because it will revert to the behaviour you wanted to discourage. Be gentle with your spoken word and your touch.

To make the recall happen, it is easier to call a dog when it is in a standing position than from its bed. Change the way you do this perhaps, make it worth investigating, like scratching the carpet with your finger. But do not look at the dog as though you're doing this to get it to come to you. When the dog does get up, encourage it over, and don't be worried in the early stages about using a bribe if necessary. You may initially use a food lure, but phase it out or it becomes a desperate bribe.

If your dog becomes demanding or over-excited again, just blank it by turning your face away and stop stroking it. If the dog continues to muck around, then gently guide it out of your space until it learns some manners. If your dog does not modify its behaviour then walk out of the room, leaving it alone for fifteen seconds and then repeat the steps above. It won't take long for your dog to realise that if they respect your space, they get you as a reward. If, when you walk out of the room, your dog bolts through, then simply shut the door behind it. This will be a good lesson for the dog to learn – you're telling it, 'When you barge past, it gets you nowhere, and I won't follow. Now you're on your own.'

When you call your dog, reward it with food and/or massage. Everything is done on your terms, not the dog's. And if you rejoin in this way, you're well ahead in the recall stakes, too. Your dog will always come to you in the home, and then the recall is established and the recall out and about is going to be infinitely easier to address.

So many times I go to homes where the dog doesn't come back when called on a walk or runs off, and the owner and dog have never done recall work at home. Invariably, the dog always gets a cuddle or interaction when it demands it. So why should your dog respond to something he's had little training in when there are much more exciting things to be sniffed and chased on the walks?

In general, people give their dog too much attention in the home and on the dog's terms, and not a lot of attention out and about. If you're boring on your walk then why would your dog want to be with you? Think of play and having fun, then your dog will think you're the best and want to be with you.

Visitors to your home should abide by your rules and not stroke the dog until you say it is fine to call it to them. Remember, not all dogs like to be molested by any old stranger – neither do you. Would you let anyone go up to a young child and make physical contact with them? No, you wouldn't, so give your dog a break – it doesn't have to be a performing seal. If he pees, cowers or lies down submissively, this is an indication that he's not having fun.

Checklist for Rejoining and Affection
Whether you have been gone for six seconds or three hours, the rules for rejoining and showing affection are exactly the same:

- If your dog is polite, then say hello and give it a brief stroke.

- Give yourself time to get your important things done then call your dog to you.

- If your dog is all over you as soon as you appear, ignore its approaches, however persistent. Guide it down if it jumps up, with no eye contact, no vocals and no emotion. If you use eye contact, the message is ambiguous.

- Get your dog to settle. You may need a home line just to stop the dog from pacing. By stopping the dog, it will enable it to calm quicker, reduce the adrenalin and result in a call over and cuddle sooner.

- After a few minutes of complete settle or avoiding responding to your dog, you can then call. Use its name to gain attention then request 'Here... good dog!' and reward when it comes gently.

- You are teaching the 'come to you' message, so don't ask your dog to sit; the dog will sit naturally when it is relaxed. You end the interaction when you are ready, and remember the deep, gentle massage with your fingertips. If you need a food reward initially, then use it, but phase it out as overuse will end up being a desperate bribe.

- All visitors must disregard your dog when they enter and only interact on your terms and your way. Let the dog sniff them – it needs time to check out the new smells. They will have their chance for a tickle later. Give the dog the opportunity just to get the information it needs first.

- Remember, do not let your dog have access to you all the time. Close doors behind you, even if only for fifteen seconds. You're saying, 'I don't need you with me and you don't need to be with me all the time. We're OK on our own and together.' This will, with a puppy, avoid any separation anxiety occurring.

- As you go about your daily business, do not keep looking at your dog. It will think it has to join in. Show your dog it can relax by simply not looking it in the eye when the task doesn't involve it.

8

Thoughtful Discipline

In every group there must be discipline in some form so that the group can function smoothly. It doesn't matter whether in the family, workplace, sports field or just in our day-to-day dealings with other people. Discipline is a set of written or unwritten rules, with the most effective form being self-discipline.

Often when humans think of discipline, enforcement is top of their list of options. The first tool at your disposal when talking about enforcing your will on a dog is physical force, either through smacking, shaking or shouting. Please don't waste your time. Apart from the fact that it is cruel, it just doesn't work. If you hit or use any other form of violence on a dog, including the dreaded 'electric shock' or 'spiked prong' collars, there will only be one of two outcomes: you will either crush the dog's spirit or you will be bitten. Neither of those outcomes will give you the result you want.

We do need ground rules, but rather than use the 'Don't ask him...tell him' or 'Just make him do it' methods, we prefer to use

'Appropriate Correction'. Why? Because we are kind, considerate, warm human beings. Oh…and because it works much better than anything else we've found.

If you constantly nag and chatter away to your dog, even if you're not telling it off but just telling it your plans for the day, then you are setting up a 'wall of sound' or 'white noise' and your dog will think, 'Here we go again…' and will switch off. If you then need to interact with it about something important, you shouldn't be surprised if it takes no notice. If you use the method as detailed, when you say your dog's name you will get an immediate and positive response rather than a 'talk to the paw'. So be clear in what you are asking your dog to do.

The Four Levels of Silent Correction

Level 1 – Face Away
Dogs use this naturally to calm situations down and to show others that they are uninterested in their approaches.

This should be used when a dog is nudging or otherwise demanding attention. Simply turn your face away, showing disinterest to its demands. You may feel it necessary to stand up as well if the dog is jumping up for your attention, particularly when you've got a mug of tea in your hand.

If and when the dog walks away, then you can call it into your space when you wish and when you're ready. This will help your dog respect your space and begin to reinforce the idea that nudging and bothering you is not always welcome whenever he feels the need to do it. If, however, your dog comes and sits and looks at you with those gorgeous eyes but at a respectful distance, then it is asking politely for a cuddle. If you have the time, then go for it!

Level 2 – Guide and Hold Your Dog Away

This should be accomplished with no speech, no eye contact and no emotion. If your dog is very persistent and pushy and hasn't taken the hint, and your tea is about to go flying then, without looking or talking to your dog, gently but firmly guide it away. It may be necessary to hold it away at arm's length by the collar until it is relaxed, then remove your hand. Repeat as many times as required, but if the dog gets more persistent, then you will have to move on to Level 3.

Level 3 – Guide and Walk Your Dog Away

Again, using no speech, eye contact and no emotion.

This is for those occasions when your dog is doing something that you really don't want it to. This is important because if you do over-react and make a big fuss of it then your dog knows how to press your buttons when it wants a reaction from you.

You can use this in a variety of situations – the dog that climbs on the furniture uninvited; the dog that persists in jumping up...the list is endless. If you don't like the behaviour, whatever it is, then calmly interrupt it.

Guide and walk your dog away at 180 degrees by its collar from the area of interest and maybe take it to its bed and hold for a second or two for it to relax, then walk away. If the dog repeats the behaviour, you move it again...and again...and again.

Alternatively, you can walk away but remain in the area.

Level 4 – Time Out

Again, using no speech, no eye contact and no emotion.

To be applied when a behaviour is completely unacceptable, from simply mouthing to biting to not getting the message from other levels of correction. Preferably remove yourselves from the room, leaving the dog on its own for fifteen seconds. This will give the dog time to think, 'Oops…shouldn't do that…I'm on my own.' Importantly, when you return to the room, say nothing to the dog and, when ready, call the dog into your space. Each time it repeats the behaviour, you extend the time-out period by doubling the time in any one session, so if you've been out for thirty seconds and the dog repeats the behaviour when you re-enter, then go out for sixty seconds.

If when you open the door to walk out of the room your dog barges through, then simply shut the door, job done – the dog is on one side on his own and you are the other. This is the ideal way to isolate in a hands-off approach.

Rarely will the dog be removed physically from the room as this can lead to more problems as you are forcing and having to be confrontational.

Do not use this method with a puppy under the age of sixteen weeks. The walk away is ample and, if they use teeth, then do say 'Ow!' and walk away. That is less effective on dogs above sixteen weeks, as they should have learnt many manners, boundaries and their bite inhibition by then. And you sound more like a wounded animal.

The time out is to be used sparingly as the very last resort, and not for little misdemeanours. So only use for painful mouthing, jumping at children and grannies and grumpiness.

Work with your dog – it needs guidance and teaching from you. And it may help to have another look at rejoining with visitors (p. 77) and the use of the home line (p. 42), Calm Walk and Calm Hold.

Remember – all four of the above methods must be undertaken using no speech, no eye contact and no emotion. If you act silently, gently, calmly but instantly, the dog will make the connection: 'Every time I perform behaviour X, I get Y. What would happen if I didn't do X?' The answer is that if the dog changes its behaviour, then it will be rewarded by being allowed to stay with you and get cuddles and the attention it craves, which is its main aim.

If you talk to and make eye contact with the dog while you are correcting it you will not get the message across loud and clear. The probability is that it would repeat the offending behaviour and you would be viewed as being confrontational, and an aggressive dog will react in a way you certainly don't want.

Your dog will learn that every action has a consequence, whether good or not so good; they will become much more respectful of your personal space. This means that the dog will still come to greet you on your return but will not leap all over you, because it now knows that if it gives you time and personal space to take your coat off or do anything else you need to do, then you will be in a position to interact with it much sooner. A well-mannered dog who wants attention from you will 'just happen' to be in your eye line looking cute.

They are giving you non-verbal signals that they are respectful and available should you wish to invite them to approach 'the throne'. If you want to invite your dog, then make warm eye contact and call it to you as detailed earlier. If, however, you don't want interaction at that time, perhaps you have a phone call to make, then just break eye contact and the message that you are busy will be received loud and clear.

As you establish respect and trust, the amount of respect you will be given will increase but things can slip if you become lazy. We teach children to say 'Please' and 'Thank you' and not to interrupt adult conversation, but sometimes they forget. You give a biscuit and they wander off without a word; you then have to remind them of their manners. The same applies to dogs. They will learn how to behave but sometimes will forget themselves. Give your dog the correct information then it will be reminded that it has to wait to be invited.

Using the Levels – Case Studies

Two different clients but the same problem – toe nipping.

The 'problem' that these two clients presented with was their dogs biting toes. This is quite a common behaviour which can range from resulting in a mild tickling action through to irritating to downright painful.

The first client's dog had started at 'tickling' but had moved to 'irritating'. Usually what happened was that the family were sitting around in the evening with bare or stockinged feet. The dog approached and sniffed, licked or gently nibbled toes. The recipient of the pedicure would giggle or pull their feet away with a laugh. What a good game. Then the human alternated the foot and gave further attention to the dog who then knew how to get his humans dancing, even when they were sitting down. Other family members laughed, which encouraged the dog who then decided that he'd do it to everybody. But when they can't concentrate on what they are doing due to the nibbling, people can suffer a severe sense of humour failure.

Now this dog was a nice little fellow but 'persistent' was his middle name. We tried moving him away as in Level 2 and then Level 3 above but to no avail. He nipped the husband's right foot yet again and so this time he was removed from the room by a home line as removing ourselves to another room would have resulted in the dog becoming more intent on the foot nipping as he now had moving targets which would be far more fun.

He came back in, waited a very short while and nipped the left foot. Out he went again. On his return, he looked at the husband, gave him a wide berth and nipped the wife's right foot. So he was removed for a third time.

When he returned, you could almost hear the cogs in his head going round. He looked at the husband as if to say, 'I did your right foot and your left foot and both times I found myself on my own.' He then looked at the wife. 'I did your right foot and got removed so, on the balance of probability, if I do your left foot...do you know what? I don't think I'll bother.' Three very short isolations, message learnt.

The second client's dog was on the painful end of the scale. We followed the same procedure and, when it became obvious that the dog wasn't going to take the hint, I said to the client, 'Next time she does that, straight out. No speech or eye contact.'

'Got it,' he said.

She nipped again and I gave the client the nod. He took her by the collar and, while leading her from the room, said, 'Right, young lady, out you go. You're a very naughty little girl.'

I said, 'No. Don't say anything.'

He replied, 'I didn't.'

'You did,' his wife chipped in.

He became angry and said, 'No I didn't.'

I thought they were going to have a domestic but then his mother-in-law stepped in and said, 'You did speak, love.'

For some reason he accepted this correction. We tried again...and again...but he couldn't stop talking. It took him eleven attempts before he made it to the door in silence. When he came in, he said, 'I just stopped myself. I bit my tongue to keep myself from speaking. It's not my fault. I'm Welsh, you see.'

Consider the different messages the two dogs were given. In the first case, unacceptable behaviour had an instant consequence. No confusion – a simple message: 'Do that and you lose the pack.' The dog was able to moderate his behaviour because he knew what was required.

The second had only confusion when being corrected. There was a wall of sound which blocked any message we were trying to get through. The dog would return to the room none the wiser and just think, 'Now where was I? Oh yes, toe biting…' We got there with the second dog but it was hard work.

9

Bonding through Play

No canine ever naturally goes for a walk in the wild – it is a waste of valuable energy. They go out to hunt or scavenge to get food and also to check boundaries to protect their patch. If on leaving base and travelling 200 metres a particularly stupid moose or dustbin steps out in front of them, then they will kill and eat it. They will then return to the den/rest/play area. They won't think that they should walk for another twenty-five miles as part of an aerobic workout. Their aim in leaving was to get food and they've achieved that with minimal effort and injury. Job done, an efficient use of time and energy.

If they don't complete the equivalent of a marathon every day, what do they do? They sleep and they play. Why do they play? For the same reasons that humans do. For fun, to keep fit, to bond with the family/team. That is why we have school or pub football teams and why groups of salesman go on paint-balling weekends – to help bond the unit. When dogs play as a group, it also helps the younger members to hone their hunting abilities, learn a range of skills and also, just as importantly, learn about each other.

It is better for you to choose the game and teach your dog the rules, then the game is in your time and is easier to stop when you've had enough.

If your dog obsessively tries to tease you with toys, with a view to you chasing it, ignore it, lift your face away until it brings the toy right up to you and then, if the dog is still holding it in its mouth – without grabbing it or making eye contact – simply guide the dog away. If it drops it in your lap, take control of it, again with no speech or eye contact.

When you have control of the toy, put it out of reach. You can, if you want to, initiate a game with the toy after a few minutes because you will be showing the dog that it's *your* decision to play now.

Don't leave a large number of toys lying around, just a couple of favourites, so the dog can entertain itself when it's on its own. Regularly change these over, say once a week, so the toy boredom factor doesn't kick in. Any special toys that you use to interact with your dog should be put away after use and only brought out by you on your terms. Toys can be trophies, toys can be status and toys can be power with some dogs, as can bones, so if you've a dog that guards toys and grumbles when anyone passes, then it should not be left in possession of these. Having said that, under no circumstances do you remove them from your dog's mouth. Shut the door on your dog and, as if by magic, it'll drop the toy. Make nothing of it if, when you enter the room, it is picked up again. When the dog does leave it alone, then remove it. No audience, no point.

An important point to remember – it is not advisable to play tugging or wrestling games with any dog. They can easily get out of hand with the wrong personality of dog.

Dogs can play as individuals or on a one-to-one basis, but the games you play with your dog are far more fun and proactive in building a friendship and bond with your dog.

Teams or groups that relax and have fun together work more efficiently. The family that plays together stays together. This is as true with dogs as with humans.

Here are a few things that you could try. Remember, a dog that doesn't play is a dog who is stressed or in some cases hasn't learnt how to. Take the stress away and it will relax, then you can show it how to play and feel comfortable in its surroundings.

Even if you have more than one dog and they play together, it is important to play games with them, too.

Sit and Lie Down

These are added to play to encourage you to teach it in a fun way. When you get your puppy, rescue dog or problem dog, we need to know that they are going to respond to you with the 'Sit', the 'Down' and the 'Heel' (with which you are inviting the dog to follow you). You can add other requests like 'Roll over', 'Give a paw', whatever you like, but the 'Sit' and 'Heel' are vital if you want to pass your canine obedience tests.

With any age of dog, ensuring it wants to be with you and chooses to be with you without pressure is paramount. We need to teach all this off-lead, so the dog is not under pressure. Ensure the lessons are short and sweet and as much about fun as learning. Do not force your dog's bottom down – repeat the request and move your hand with food held uppermost and the head comes up and the bottom down. If the dog just walks backwards then place the dog with a wall or cupboard behind it.

This doesn't stop you taking your dog to play in the park and socialise with pups of the same age and size. Ask your vet if there are others in the area who like to come and play. If you have an eight- to fifteen-week-old pup this is a great opportunity to introduce it to puppies of the same age. And get the dog to Respond to Recall (p. 97) when there are distractions of a canine nature and strangers around as well, ideally in an enclosed garden/area. A dog over sixteen weeks is not strictly a puppy any more; it is coming into adolescence and, if bite inhibition hasn't been addressed by other owners of these pups, you're setting your pup up for a fall.

With 'Lie down', draw the dog under a chair/low table initially, so it can get it right without you having to force it.

When your dog has got 'Sit', then add in 'Stay'. Put your hand up and step one pace away quickly backwards, praise and reward. Slowly but surely, increase the time taken and don't become irritated if your dog gets up because it wants to be with you and feels vulnerable or confused. Be patient. Place the dog in a sit again and persevere, but keep lessons short and fun. Quit while you're ahead.

It's worth noting that I have never seen another dog ask another to sit or stay or heel. They follow and stay with each other for safety and teamwork. My own dogs will sit when asked, but I never ask them to. The only request I give is 'Here'. I never use all the common, 'human-focused' requests to control a dog, I want my dogs to exercise self-control and look to me, rather than me micro-managing their world. They are just good games to play and useful to have up your sleeve to pass canine control tests.

Fetch

If your dog is big and bouncy then it would be a good idea to start this exercise when the dog is calm. Using a ball – or any other item that's safe and might appeal to your dog – maybe roll it instead of throwing it. If your dog is not an enthusiastic ball/toy player, you will have to encourage it by waggling the toy in front of the dog and exciting it a bit before you throw. Try different toys – smelly socks – anything to get your dog to want to do it.

So your dog doesn't bring it back. If it goes off and plays its own game and does not try seemingly to involve you in any way, try playing footie with the ball to encourage your dog to pick it up and, when it does, run away and call your dog. Then, when the dog gives it to you or drops it near you, throw it again. If, however, you end up playing a game of chase and it really has no intention of giving it to you then, if you are outside, walk inside (or vice versa) and, more often than not, the dog will drop it and come to see where you have gone. 'Why are you not watching me? I was trying to get you to play my game...' will be the likely reaction. The dog has lost its audience and you're not begging him to play. That's not what your dog expected.

With a dog such as this, it is ideal to start the game off inside or make an 'alley way' for it, so the dog can't run off and it has to bring the toy towards you. When the dog turns around with the ball in its mouth, then turn your body sideways and clap your hands to encourage it. By turning yourself sideways you are not in a challenging position with eye-to-eye contact (just the odd glance). When the dog does come with the ball, reward and throw again...and so the game continues. Quit while you are ahead; three separate fetches is plenty to begin with. Make it happen by putting on your most exciting voice and being really enthusiastic with your body language.

If, when the dog comes with the ball and does not release it, offer a swap – a piece of chicken maybe. The next time the dog goes for the ball, it may drop it halfway and run for the food reward. He's thinking, 'Forget the ball – I want that chicken!' Well, unlucky, mate, the deal is you bring me the ball and then you get a reward. No such thing as a free lunch. In this instance, go up to the ball and kick it around, encouraging the dog to pick it up and bring it to you. Remember to crouch side-on as it approaches and not too much eye contact as the dog will lock on your eyes and stand back with an 'It's mine!' look on its face. Your eyes are a challenge to it, rather than a 'Please give it to me'.

As you progress, you can make this game more interesting by throwing the ball into longer vegetation so your dog has to use its nose and maybe help from you to find it. Keep the game interesting so you work as a team and give it more to think about. Dogs will get bored with repetitive games – you throw the ball, they bring it back... you throw the ball again and they bring it back... you throw for a third time and the dog may well look at you as if to say, 'OK, you don't want it, I understand!' and then wander off to please itself somewhere else. These dogs are bright guys and you need to keep them guessing, change the game, hide the ball and work together as a team to find it. Be exciting and you will get them excited.

Other dogs will become obsessed with games of fetch; it is repetitive and easy, so get them thinking more by getting them to work using their noses to find hidden toys with you.

If you have two dogs, one will generally get the ball before the other and, before you know it, the slower one will give up and stop even trying. So ensure you play so they can all get involved and no one is left out. It may even mean holding one by the collar while you throw or play Find with the other.

'Follow Me'

Make the heel work into a game of 'Follow Me' – run around the garden getting your dog to chase you and if it jumps up, stop and wait until all is calm and then start off again. Sprint, change your direction, walk, stop, change, trot, stop, walk, change... and so on, as exaggerated physically and vocally as you can. If you are having fun you can bet your bottom dollar that your dog is, too. With a very bouncy dog, you have to calm things down, but you can still be fun.

Try some homemade agility courses by putting some obstacles up to jump over or some cones to weave in and out of and enjoy. In the house, lay the broom on the floor, along with an old box and chairs to weave round and jump over.

Further Suggestions for Learning through Play

Once you have a solid grounding in your relationship with your dog, you may want to get involved in other enjoyable activities. Before you take your dog along and sign up to a dog club, ask if you can just attend on your own and sit in and watch one evening. Any club worth its salt will be happy to agree in order to attract new members. Decide what sort of club you want to join – do you want to take part in a competitive way or just for fun? Many clubs, such as agility, cater for both, while others are more focused. Remember, you are doing this for enjoyment, so take your time to find the club and activity that best suits you and your dog.

Agility

Great fun and good for fitness in both dog and handler as well as promoting bonding. Do not start this until your dog is at least a year old – most agility places won't accept a dog until it is eighteen months old – to avoid damaging joints that are not fully formed. There is nothing stopping you laying this out at home or in the garden with makeshift obstacles.

Flyball

A very fast sport, quickly burning off energy, but it is repetitive and can cause some dogs to be ball obsessed.

Tricks

There are some great books out there to explain how to teach tricks to your dog. This is great for their brain and huge fun for both of you.

These and many other pastimes are out there for you and your dog. You may, however, just want to go for a stroll in the park together. Whatever your choice, as long as your dog is in no doubt as to who is taking the lead, you will both be happy.

I have said this many times, but it's always worth repeating: wherever you are with your dog, it's *who you're with* that is important, not *where* you are, so be fun and have fun. We see so many people walking their dogs and having no interaction whatsoever.

It's also good to remind yourself sometimes that it is just as important to let your dog do other doggy things like sniffing and finding out about where it is and what's about. So do remember to pause and take in the view occasionally while your dog can stop and sniff. We so often forget to sense what's around us or above us, as the sights and smells we miss are often worth catching. So remember to enjoy just being out there with your mate.

10

Common Behavioural Problems

As mentioned already, it never matters what your dog does, only what you do in response. If you make nothing of something (but be proactive) it will be just that – nothing. But you must be calm, confident, convincing and consistent to make it happen.

Sudden Behavioural Changes

If your dog displays any behaviour that is not normal for it, such as asking to go out in the early hours to toilet, or not toileting at the regular time, or perhaps just not looking its normal self, then it may mean that there is an underlying medical issue. Even if you cannot claim to be medically trained in any way, there are some things that should make you think, 'Is everything as it should be healthwise with my dog?'

For example, the onset of epilepsy might be flagged up if your dog has suddenly started to show signs of aggression towards family members or visitors, or have 'blank' moments or shakes for no apparent reason. If your dog is usually 'buzzy' and is then rather quiet or vice versa, then take a trip to the vet's. If it has grown up and has gradually become more of a hooligan as it matures, then it is most probably a purely behavioural issue. Dogs can't tell us if they don't feel well, but they are able to indicate that something is wrong.

Teaching the Recall

Before recalling your dog, make sure you're worth coming back to. Are you angry or permanently grumpy? If your idea of getting your best friend to come back to you is to bellow like a sergeant major because you think it makes it sound like you're in charge, think again. Just as bad as the macho roar is the boring bleat. If you're not worth coming back to, then why should your dog bother? Motivate yourself, be welcoming, lighten your voice but, most of all, get a pulse!

Recall starts at home and, if you do your rejoining correctly, you're almost there. You've only got the outside world to tackle now.

Before you'll get great recall on your walks, the exercise has to be learnt at home. The other important necessity is for you to have really good lead work, with your dog looking to you and turning with you naturally as you move along.

There is no point racing to the park with your dog pulling and then releasing a dog pumped with adrenalin and expecting it to hear you or respond to you when you call it. So get recall and lead work really solid at home and in the garden.

Be inventive if you're struggling with recall. It is always easier to call a dog when it is standing than snuggled in its bed, so take the opportunity when you can and initially always give a great food reward and massage. The food reward must be phased out as you move forward or it becomes a bribe and the dog will only come back if you're loaded with chicken!

If you stand or crouch side-on, this will help, too. Drop your eye contact every now and again, then the dog can't stare you in the eye and indicate 'Talk to the paw' again.

A great asset is another game, such as fetch and seeking games. If you play these at home and the dog loves them, then play them on your walk, too, and you'll keep its attention.

Don't let your dog off-lead and cross your fingers. Attach a long line – nine metres should be long enough, as you could end up having to untangle miles of spaghetti with anything much longer.

Get to your destination beautifully together, and don't always let your dog off the lead at the same place. For some dogs, the sound of the clip on the lead acts like a trigger that launches them into 'I'm free!' rampage mode. So don't take it off, just let it drop and add the long line on to it.

Rather than sending your dog off to play, just simply change direction. By sending your dog away, you're saying, 'Occupy yourself, I'm busy with other things.' By having a line attached when you call your dog and it doesn't return, simply stand on the line and turn the dog to face you by walking away, then recall it again. When the dog comes, it gets a reward, food and game.

A lot of dogs give up returning to their owners at about six months old, because they have found more interesting things with which to occupy themselves. If you're not much fun, or when you call your dog you simply turn and walk and don't interact with it, then who could blame them?

Start in locations that have little or no distractions and move on to others slowly but surely. Ensure that your dog isn't too far away, as distance means blocked ears initially. Dogs – as we do – become so focused on what they are concentrating on that they aren't ignoring the request; they simply don't hear it. The aim here is for your dog to tune in to you. Get everything working well close to you, and give your dog more distance as it gets it. Too far too soon and you won't be helping it to succeed. Don't just cross your fingers and hope, because hope won't make it happen... we've all tried that one and failed.

The not returning when called makes me think of my children engrossed in a film. It's not them ignoring me, they are not being bad, they are just too fixed and involved in the film so they physically don't hear me. I have to get closer and call them to bring them back in the moment and to me.

As they have grown up, they are more aware of their surroundings and others and don't get so drawn away into their own little worlds. It all comes with teaching, growing up and practice.

Recall with Two Dogs

If you call one dog and the other comes as well as, or instead of the recalled dog, disregard the interloper, maybe even hold it away by its collar if it insists on butting in. Only interact with the dog that you've called. You are the leader and decide who may approach the throne. It is also important that dogs realise that they are individuals.

The dog who always pushes the others out of the way will learn some self-control from this and will get nothing if it behaves like that. The bonus also is that the less assertive one will get some attention and feel braver, knowing that you have got the measure of the one that thinks he's top dog.

By saying anything to the interloper you are acknowledging it first; it's got your attention and job done as far as that dog's concerned. You have deferred to it.

Separation Anxiety

If a dog is confident in your abilities to look after both it and yourself – because it has accepted that you cannot make poor decisions – it will trust any course of action you decide upon, and therefore will be relaxed with or without you. The dog feels safe in the knowledge that you have taken (and proved your worth in) the role of decision-maker. It does not feel pressured by the need to take care of itself or you – you are now trusted never to put your dog in a dangerous situation.

If, however, your dog feels responsible for you, then it is in his nature to follow and be there for you, either in a nurturing way, as with a mother watching over a puppy, or as a mate watching over his partner. In this latter case, the dog's determination to be with you at all times can progress to aggression toward anyone who gets between either of you.

Another cause of separation anxiety can occur if you have allowed the dog to follow you constantly from a puppy. Just as a child who has never been encouraged to leave its mother's side, the dog may become so clingy that being on its own will be very uncomfortable.

We know dogs are sociable animals, and that they evolved as members of family packs as the best means of survival, so to be alone is not natural for them. You need to create a mindset where they feel happy in their own skin, with or without you.

To achieve this, follow the advice below, paying particular attention to the section on taking the sting out of leaving.

If your dog is relaxed and showing no signs of stress, do not mistake its natural preference to be in close proximity to you with separation anxiety – just as you choose to be in close company with a loved one, so does your dog. The acid test is if the dog is content to be alone when it is necessary for you to leave the house without it, or you can be in another room with a closed door behind you and it is happy there. If the dog accepts this without stress, you do not have a problem – just enjoy the fact that when you are there, you are the one it chooses to be near.

Some people suggest – and no doubt you will have heard this more than once – 'Oh, get another dog…that'll sort it out.' Well, in most cases it doesn't, because the dog may not have the fear of being on its own, it has simply become clingy towards you for its own protection or protecting you. You need to look at the whole picture to be able to establish exactly what the trigger is.

There are different levels of separation anxiety – those dogs who don't like to be in another room when you are in and are fine when you're out. Others will howl or bark for five minutes then stop, and there are others that go on and on and on when you are out.

Simply changing your routine and stopping the triggers will suffice many times, but more often than not it is the following process that sorts it. And, believe me, it can be very tedious, but worth it.

You may have been advised just to crate your dog; this will mean your kitchen won't be wrecked but the dog still has a big problem. But don't worry – we can sort this problem out in a proactive way that causes the least stress for both you and your dog.

As noted previously, playing classical music softly is a very useful tool; it will help you, along with the simple instructions below, to bring calm to your troubled furry friend.

Taking the Sting out of Leaving

We first have to desensitise your dog to your every movement. In our busy lives, we're always doing one thing then moving on to the next – getting up, making coffee, going to work…and so on. So we get up to go somewhere. If you look at your dog when you get up, you're inviting it to join you. Let the poor bloke have some rest! Each and every time you're asking your dog to be with you, it's got no idea why, but you obviously can't function without it. This is sending you down that slippery slope to a dog that can't be without you.

You have to break those habits. Remember, just because you do A doesn't mean B will follow. And it's important you follow the rules

strictly – do not speak to your dog, or look at your dog while completing these activities. Making eye contact is to invite your dog to join
you in your chosen activity. Each number stage will take a lot of time
and effort for a very stressed dog. Don't think you can rattle through
the seven stages in a day and get a result. If you're good at this, it is
possible to cure separation anxiety in a week and sometimes far less.

1. When you're sitting comfortably (wherever you are) in the
   home, make sure you can move around in your chair without
   your dog reacting.

2. Make sure you can stand up and sit down, without your dog
   jumping to attention. Usually when we stand up we are going
   to do something. Well, just stand up and stretch, then sit again.

3. Walk to the door and back.

4. Rattle the door knob and sit down, each time making sure the
   dog settles on your return – you may have to use a Calm Hold
   (p. 57) or Calm Walk (p. 59) to make this happen.

5. Then leave the room for two seconds and return and sit, each
   time not looking at or acknowledging the dog's reaction. You
   are showing your dog that you can come and go without it
   having to worry or react.

6. Increase the time outside the door by seconds at first.

7. As you increase your time away (very gradually), if you have
   the facilities then leave by one door and return by another.
   All this is done with no eye contact, vocals or emotion.

If your dog gets up and has trouble settling between your movements,
then just guide the dog to its bed and use a Calm Hold until it relaxes

and lies down. Then continue after a short time so it relaxes further. By doing this, you are showing your dog that there really isn't an issue. You are completely relaxed and therefore it can be, too.

You will need a huge amount of patience and time in some cases, so stick with it and you and your dog will be rewarded.

If when you return from any of the exits the dog is overly distressed, it means you have been out too long. Go back to the period of time that the dog coped well in your absence and move on from there. You will get to a stage when the dog does not react to your movement and stays relaxed wherever it may be. And don't be misled by the idea that your dog can only be relaxed in its bed.

It's also good practice to use your doors so your dog doesn't have the opportunity to follow you everywhere. You will be showing it that you do not need a bodyguard – you can look after yourself.

The reason you exit so gradually is that the dog doesn't have time to get too upset, and when you return your dog will settle quicker as its adrenalin will not have shot up off the scale.

Do the Taking the Sting out of Leaving until you are so bored with it you could post a rotten egg through my letterbox ... but it's worth it if your dog sleeps happily.

You are really showing the dog that it is fine on its own and so are you – you can go about your daily business without being followed all the time and your dog can start to enjoy true relaxation, only having to get up when really necessary – for a cuddle, a walk or a play, a potter to the water bowl or garden to lie in the sun.

What is also helpful is to combine these measures with classical music playing in the background, and lavender scent in your dog's sleeping area. But do not rely on any of these gadgets as a solution on their own – you have to work at it.

You can easily incorporate this method into daily life as with everything else. For instance, if you are in the sitting room and wish to make a cuppa, then break it down into three or four steps. Go out of the room and shut the door and put the kettle on, then return, disregarding your dog's approaches. When settled, go out of the room again and get a cup from the cupboard, return as above and then go out and put a tea bag in the cup. Return, then go back out and, at this stage, you may have to boil the kettle again! All in a good cause though – effective dog training. It's a very long-winded way of making a simple cuppa but you do get one in the end. You have also taught your dog a valuable lesson – you don't need them with you all the time.

If there is more than one person in the household, when the family are all seated around the TV in the evening, then do take turns and practise taking the sting out of leaving individually. By doing this, you are all showing your dog that you can take care of yourselves. If one member leaves the room and your dog is anxious and/or pacing, any member still in the room can gently go up to the dog and take it by the collar, then draw it close for a Calm Hold without a word. You'll be showing it that you have no concerns about that person leaving and the dog will feel your calmness.

As calmness sets in, you can extend this to leaving the house. From sitting reading the paper, you can get up and walk out of the front door. When you return initially after a few seconds out, sit down, pick up the paper and carry on reading just as if you'd been to the bathroom. You can extend the time before returning, or leave by the front door and return via the back door. Several family members could leave at once and return at ten-second intervals or you could even time it so that some come in the front at the same time as others arrive via the back. You are only limited in what you do by your imagination. You have to show your dog that you can go where you like, whenever you like, for as long as you like.

The reason we do this in silence is that we confuse the dog if we say anything. We want it to see what we are doing and not feel it has any part to play. Put a dog right in silence so it begins to think for itself and modifies its own behaviour. We must always remember that dogs don't talk, they watch and learn by example. We also learn by example, we trust by example. Just because someone says that they are the best at their job, you won't believe them until they really prove it to you.

Shut doors behind you even if it is only for thirty seconds. You're saying, 'I don't need you with me.' When you open it, you are indicating that your dog can come in if it likes. If you're needy and expect your dog to be with you every step, then it will know you're needy and it'll end up needy too... so everyone is needy and no one gets a rest.

Mouthing

Mouthing is wholly unacceptable as a puppy or adult – dogs' jaws are strong and there may be a time when they put too much pressure on and hurt. This is especially important if you have children or come into contact with them. Remember, mouthing the wrong person could be construed as a bite and then you're in trouble.

Puppies learn not to bite hard. Well-known dog trainer Dr Ian Dunbar states that it is up to sixteen weeks of age that they learn their bite inhibition, which is why he runs puppy classes up to an age of sixteen weeks. If a pup hasn't learnt this by then, training takes on a different tack.

If a puppy mouths or nibbles (aged up to sixteen weeks), shout 'Ow!' then walk away, showing and sounding your displeasure as its sibling and mother would. When the pup is minding its own business, then recall it again to you and stroke calmly with quiet, soothing vocals and you're more likely to stop the unacceptable behaviour quicker. If you are over-zealous in your stroking and/or over-verbal, then you will simply wind the pup up and the result will be mouthing, nipping or jumping up. If you have an excitable dog, you will have to learn to be calmer around it – it is very easy to over-excite a dog without meaning to.

With an older dog, above sixteen weeks, then the shout of 'Ow!' will sound like a wounded animal. Be the strong, silent one and walk out of the room as in the fourth level of Silent Correction (p. 82).

Smiling Dogs

Some dogs do smile – they have learnt to mimic the human and the mimic usually gets a positive reaction from humans, so it's well worth doing from a dog's point of view. People find the smile endearing, likening it to the human smile of welcome. The smiling dog has no fight on its mind, there is no growl or fearsome eyes or aggressive stance.

Also be aware, however, that in general when dogs show their teeth – their weapons – it's most definitely a warning. When I call a strange dog to me, I do make a point of not showing my teeth. I smile with closed lips and a kind voice and very little eye contact. Then there is no doubt that I'm a friend.

Barging through Doorways

If your dog barges past you, it has no respect in the slightest for you or your personal space. Naturally, if a dog respects another it will stand aside to let the other take priority through a gap. Look at your own dogs; is there one that is grumpy at doorways? Is there one that always stands aside for the other? Do they all pile in together on an equal footing? They probably show respect to each other... it's now time to get them to respect you.

I will open a door for an older person and stand aside – that's respectful. I was taught to be respectful. We need to teach our dogs this same respect. We do not want the dog rushing past, potentially knocking you sideways, coffee cups flying and granny on the floor with a fractured femur.

Remember, dogs want to be with us, so we always use this to our advantage. First, use the doors in your house – stop living open plan (unless you have no choice because you have no doors!) When you get up and move to another room, open the door, own the door, *don't* step to the side, or you are showing respect to your dog; it will only be interpreted as a 'Please, you first!' attitude.

So you open the door, but do not ask your dog to sit or stay there. We want your dog to start thinking about you, not what you say. Make sure no one is in the room you wish to enter. If the dog rushes past into the next room, do not follow your dog in, just calmly shut the door, so you are one side and the dog on the other. I'd love to see the look on your dog's face the first time this happens! Then after about fifteen seconds, open the door, stand aside and, with no speech or eye contact, face away. Your dog will come back in. You may have to step away from the door to allow this to happen.

It will not take long for the dog to realise you are not a follower and for the dog to start thinking where it should be and who needs to respect whom. Do this indoors off-lead, and then on-lead you can practise at your front door for when you start off on your outside walks. Your dog will look to you, think about you and stop being a barger.

Jumping Up

Why does your dog jump up at you or at visitors or on a walk at people you meet? They are trying to get attention.

It may be a nervous reaction or a 'Stay away!' manoeuvre as with a Boxer I once met, one step away from a more aggressive measure. We probably didn't discourage it as a puppy and teach it the correct way to approach. If you or your children were to do this, then you would not be very well accepted into society. So why do we let dogs get away with it? I'm sure not everyone is pleased when their best suit has to visit the dry cleaner's, not to mention those poor people who are afraid of dogs, who have to endure such boisterous physical contact with your four-legged friend.

With a puppy, this is their natural behaviour when their mother returns, encouraging her to regurgitate her food by licking her mouth. Our heads are a lot higher than a canine mother's and therefore they jump higher. If we encourage this behaviour, they learn they can get attention – good or bad, it's all attention, and it then turns into demanding behaviour. The dog has no self-control and is just calling the shots. Who's in control when you re-enter the house or a room? Your dog is if it asks for attention, particularly in a boisterous manner, and gets it.

If this is happening to you, whenever you see the behaviour, simply (without a word) push the dog off gently either with your arm or leg and say nothing, while not engaging in any eye contact. Repeat this if the dog does not get the message after a few times. You could then try clipping a home line on your dog and put it into a silent walk to concentrate its mind. This will get the dog to look to you, follow you; remember, the creator of movement has the power. Then calmly stand still, drop the line and walk away. You may have to repeat this a couple of times before your dog gets it. As a last resort, walk out of the room without a word for ten seconds of quiet behind the nearest door. Re-enter when the dog is quiet and repeat if necessary. It is a battle of wits and determination – if you are determined, you will make it happen. If you say anything, whether it's in a positive or negative tone, the dog's got your attention.

If we are talking puppies (under sixteen weeks), then guide it down and stroke it with four feet on the ground.

If you're in the park, then your dog should be on a lead and you can guide and walk it away. If the dog runs after people and jumps on them in the park, then it should not be off a lead whether it is a short one or a long line, until it has learnt some manners, can be recalled and focuses on you.

If when you walk into a room your dog doesn't mug you while you hang your coat up and make a cup of tea, then you can call it over for a cuddle. In this way, the reward is given in the form of a recall and cuddle for not getting in your way when it's not convenient. The message is now clear that your dog will get called over quicker for a cuddle or a play as a result.

People often say that when they tell their dog to get 'down' it does, but they always have to say it. Wouldn't it be lovely if you didn't have to say that any more and the dog respected your personal space without a word? And what a relief that it's no longer springing into action at a moment's notice.

On-lead Pulling

So off you go for your daily walk, your dog going over-the-top when the lead comes out and you have to rugby tackle it to get the thing on in the first place! You've started your walk off in the house with all guns blazing before you even venture out of the door. You're heading for failure, right from the word go.

So you go from a rugby tackle to tug of war in seconds. This is a long way from the enjoyable breath of fresh air you had planned. So why does your dog pull?

- Generally because we haven't taught them otherwise, and we let them.

- We may have tried when they were young and then gave up.

- You may have a nervous dog on the lead that hugs the fences and hedges as you walk along the road; it may be reluctant to go out initially, then pull all the way home, the place he never wanted to leave in the first place.

- Your dog may have found that the quicker it gets you to the park, the quicker it can have fun.

- Your dog may simply want to be out there in front leading the way and keeping a look-out for food (whether chasing rabbits or picking up an old burger wrapper) and danger.

Pulling does hurt – both you and your dog (although if you have a Yorkshire terrier, then probably not you). It is also not a lot of fun for either of you. You need to be able to show your dog that it's you it needs to follow, to watch, and that being by your side is not only fun but a safe place to be. Heeling is taught as a 'Follow Me' game, building the elements slowly but surely, starting at home in a calm environment off-lead, where there are no distractions or concerns. You can both relax and have fun learning who follows whom.

The problem will also occur because, when we go for a walk, we go in a straight line and pay little attention to the dog. By heading off and keeping to a straight line, the dog logs on to your direction and speed and logs off you.

Don't have your mobile or book in one hand and dog in the other. Be engaging and fun, get your dog's eye contact, be inventive, change your direction or cross the road every now and again. Stop regularly, and always praise and reward when the dog gets it right. If it pulls in front, stop – it can't pull if you don't follow! When your dog is at your side, praise and reward. Make it into a fun interaction and a game of 'Follow Me'.

When you practise heel work it is generally done in a fairly artificial environment like the village hall, and this can become the only venue when the dog does walk to heel, often reverting to previous poor behaviour when leaving the hall. We also come across situations where we cannot get the 'Heel' as there is a distraction the dog is more aware of than being by your side, whether that be danger, scent sniffing or other four-legged animals such as rabbits (food on legs to a dog). Keep the dog thinking about you and not concerning itself with everything else. Take a look at the section on the walk (p. 61). Remember, stopping is as important as walking to get the dog to focus on you.

If it helps, have a squeaky toy handy to help keep his attention. And try our Happy At Heel Harness that has had rave reviews in the UK. The harness attaches across the front of the dog and enables the owner to teach their dog to focus on them and walk gently by their side. By having the lead attached in this way, if the dog pulls forward it is corrected gently with little effort. If your dog lunges, it is guided round to face the owner rather than the object of interest and, in so doing, attention is put back on to the handler. This shows the dog, in a stress-free way, that it is not in control. By quickly and effortlessly turning your dog, you can then walk off in the direction you choose as though nothing has happened.

Very quickly your dog will learn that lunging or pulling forward is pointless and they will start to look to you for guidance. You lead the walk, not your dog.

Excessive Barking

The morning post comes flying through the door. 'What is it? Is it going to kill us? I'll bark, that'll show him…I'll kill the paper!' thinks the dog. Postmen and paperboys are always fair game for dogs. They come at more or less the same time every day, they rattle the letterbox and poke stuff through it. The dog develops a routine as well. At 7.05 a.m., the paperboy arrives and the dog barks. 'Clear off!' And he does. The dog thinks, 'That told him...he won't try that again!'

At 8.30 a.m., the postman arrives and we have a repeat performance, where the dog successfully repels the perceived attack. Of course, neither paperboy nor postman learn their lesson and tomorrow morning they'll be back again and up to their old tricks, which really provokes the dog and raises its stress levels. Won't these humans ever learn?

It is as straightforward as that. It's easy to forget that dogs do not understand our world and everything we do in it – there is no reason why they should. We have to show them that post really isn't a problem for us and the postman or visitor hasn't come here to kill either. If we make nothing of something, it will become nothing; in the same way, if we make something of nothing it will become something.

If we shout and scream, 'Stop it!' the dog just thinks you're joining in, too, and bounces around more or barks more and you end up with a hoarse voice and a red face!

Let's approach it from a different angle and show the dog our gratitude for warning us of impending danger, then *we* take charge of the situation in a cool, calm and collected manner so that the dog sees that we are dealing with what he indicated as danger and placing him in the back seat. 'What a relief!' the dog thinks.

So for your dog to bark at the door is a good thing, a warning that there's something about. However, to continue to bark and bark is not only irritating to the next-door neighbours and challenging for you, it is a dog in a huge panic, not knowing what to do and trying its hardest to ward off danger. Even if you can't see or hear anything that started it off, remember that your dog's sense of smell and hearing are far, far greater than ours. Be the adult – take over and show your dog that all is fine and you can cope and he can chill out. Have another look at the Checklist for Dealing with Danger' in (p. 45).

Attention Barking

If you can, ignore it. Calm the situation down by turning your face away. Walk out of the room leaving your dog behind and re-enter when it is quiet. If it is too much and you have neighbours banging on the walls, then I suggest you put your dog into a Calm Walk – no speech, no eye contact, no emotion (p. 59). Say nothing to the dog and repeat as necessary. When the dog gives up and disregards you in the room, then recall it for a cuddle and reward.

Do remember that in all these methods, you will have to allow your dog as many times as it takes to get it right. It may well try again the next evening and the next, but until you get your way, do not give in. If you give in, then your dog has won and it has your attention on its terms.

If you give your dog a chew to entertain itself at this stage then all you are doing is re-enforcing the behaviour. It's got your attention and every time it barks at you, you respond with food – it's got you wrapped around its little paw. The dog has trained you to respond to its demands.

Car Concerns

Many dogs have trouble travelling in cars, ranging from mild restlessness through anxiety to full-blown hysteria. By using the techniques in this book you will be able to resolve these issues. Even in extreme cases, you can overcome your dog's negative perception of travelling in a vehicle. Importantly, you are not alone!

We have a group of friends and colleagues in the Southern Hemisphere doing similar work to us. In 2008, during the horrendous Victoria bush fires which left humans and animals dead or injured and homes and environments destroyed, many groups (including Dog Listeners) got heavily involved in rescue work with the 'Fire Dogs' as they became known. They'd lost their homes and maybe their families; some had a range of burns or other injuries; and all were traumatised. Even if the whole family had survived, they had nowhere to live, and were struggling to look after their dogs.

The rescue teams travelled countless miles to collect dogs and take them to a place of safety where they could be worked with to de-traumatise them, keep them safe and, in the happiest of cases, reunite them with their original families.

Of course, in such rescue circumstances, one of the first things that had to be done was to get the dog into a vehicle – easier said than done. We are talking about terrified and maybe fearfully aggressive animals here.

Rescuers in Australia wrote a simple step-by-step guide for use in these situations which, with their kind permission, I have used to supplement our own tried and tested methods:

- Lead-walk your dog to the car, making a point of changing direction and stopping a few times before you even go near the car and put the focus back on you – this reminds the dog who is making the decisions and, in this instance, getting close to and into the car.

- It also makes a huge difference if you take a few minutes to bring the dog's adrenalin down before it gets into the car.

- Be careful not to fall into the trap of trying to pacify a dog with words, no matter how soothing. So avoid patting, stroking or even looking at it.

- Eye contact from a dog you don't know may be perceived as

confrontational or even tip a very stressed dog over the edge. Eye contact is the beginning of communication and, if a dog is concerned, then the eye contact from you is going to confirm its thoughts, no matter what comes out of your mouth.

- If you're transporting a dog you don't know, give it as much personal space as possible.

- If it is your own dog who has car trouble, then using the Calm Hold (p. 57) for a short period in the back of the car is maybe all it needs.

- Having the dog on a long lead, no matter where or how far back in the car it is, enables you to put the slightest tension on it at certain times and this can stop the dog from over-reacting.

- Just having the lead on your shoulder seems to calm some dogs as they can feel your energy down the lead. The lead also allows you to apply a gentle, calming pressure if necessary.

- Stopping ten minutes down the road, pulling over and opening up the back and just sitting next to the dog and letting it have a drink if need be can help reduce stress levels. This can quite quickly help dogs that might have started 'stressed panting', as it can help break their stressful mindset and then continue without panting.

- Dogs in covered crates with the crate safely anchored also helps reduce stress when travelling with a dog in the car – they have no visuals and can hide.

- Maybe try to use newspaper to block out the side windows so you still have rear vision but the dog won't see that 'flashing past' effect as you drive along.

- Lots of dogs do much better if they are low to the bottom of the car in a foot-well.

- Tethering a dog in a good car harness so can't run or spin also helps.

- Changing the location of the dog in the car also can make a huge difference.

I hope something here gives you an idea you can try. As you can see, the story is always the same, whatever the problem you're dealing with. Keep it calm and don't put stress on the dog – they've had enough of that already. Just be that rock that silently says everything is in hand, there's no danger any more.

Chasing Animals

As far as your dog is aware when out and about walking with you, you are out on the hunt. But you have done the weekly shopping and you don't need any extras! However, your dog doesn't know that.

Your dog is most probably having a great time but it is out there in front taking the lead and you are dutifully following it. Calling and calling your dog, who does not respond, is only reassuring it that you are there and, when it wants to, it can find you easily.

A lot of dogs will look back to see you are there and then carry on in the direction they were going. They are happy in the knowledge that you are trying to keep up with them on their hunt, regardless of the fact that you are going blue in the face shouting for them to return.

We need your dog to be tuned in to you, so it follows you on your walk and not the other way around. If you don't feel like a rabbit or chicken-chasing session, then the hunt should be called off. Leader says, 'No!' and then carries on for a lovely, relaxed walk. Rather than your dog on his walk and you on yours, wouldn't it be great to be together and enjoy the company of each other?

Make sure that your lead work and recall are perfect at home and anywhere else you walk your dog before you try off-lead where there are distractions. Build it up gradually, and don't expect the recall to be perfect in the middle of the park or rabbit warren even if it is perfect at home. Do not let your dog off a long line hoping it has got the message – work at it.

When your dog looks back, change direction and encourage it to follow, maybe break into a run…be fun and maybe hide. Your dog will come and find you. Keep it guessing.

Marking and Defecating in the House

Puppies soil in the house when we first get them but, within a few weeks, we hope to have taught the new puppy the correct place to relieve itself – outside in an appropriate location. Both dogs and puppies relieve themselves at fairly predictable times: after sleeping; after eating; or at the beginning of a walk, for example.

They will also give you a signal if you are alert enough to spot it. The easiest dogs are the ones who go to the back door and give a gentle bark or maybe a scratch. The quieter dog might just sit by the door hoping that a human will read the signal. Younger or less confident dogs might appear restless and pace in the house. If the dog starts to circle, then it is running out of options and can't wait. With young puppies, as with young children, the connection to the brain that alerts them to the need for a pee break is not made. Even when the connection is made, puppies – like children – can become so engrossed in the game they're playing that accidents happen. The best way to tackle this is as always to take the stress away from both you and the dog. Maximise your chances of success and, in so doing, make it possible to legitimately praise your puppy.

Each time the puppy has eaten, do take it outside. When it performs one or the other, then reward with food and praise. If a puppy has woken up from sleep, then take it outside to relieve itself and food reward when it does what is required. If he has an accident in the house, say nothing and just clean it up. Puppy will think, 'I get nothing in the house for my present but get praise and reward outside...' and it will soon learn. If you tell it off when it's offered a gift inside, it may wet itself out of fear or think, 'Hey, that's another way to get attention.'

You wouldn't punish a young child or granny for having an accident. They didn't mean to – it's uncomfortable and maybe embarrassing for them, so why compound their misery? They grow up, they get bladder control and they're fine. It's all a game of patience and understanding. Then you get old and you lose it – so be warned!

Now with mature dogs this is an anxiety problem (unless it has a bladder infection or bowel problem). Some dogs hate going outside; some will even (having gone for a long walk) wait until they get home and inside until they perform. If a dog has to have its wits about it while out and about, ready to spring into action at any moment, it can't relax and do its business and you wouldn't be able to either. If you were to take the luxury of relieving yourself, you would be immobilised and therefore vulnerable. Also, if you're tense, then you can't relax enough to perform anyway. Dogs are individuals and some, if really anxious, will have loose motions when out on a walk where this may not be the case in the back garden.

Some dogs urinate when visitors arrive – this is a sign of being nervous or anxious. If only your visitors would leave the dog alone and not invade its space, then it wouldn't happen. Some dogs do this with their owners, often if the owners go into a dog's space rather than call the dog to them.

Other dogs may do this when you're out – a sign either of separation anxiety or that you've left them too long. Take a look at the section on Separation Anxiety (p. 100).

Excessive Marking on the Walk

Dogs mark to tell other dogs that they've been there and that it's their territory, even though we know it is not really anyone's territory – it is shared. Your dog, by leaving messages like this constantly on a walk, is a dog with a job and not truly relaxing into the fun and enjoyment of the exercise. It's too busy letting everyone else know it's about. The higher the scent mark, the greater chance it has to catch the wind and travel further. We've all seen dogs that will almost do a handstand to get their mark higher up a lamp-post to ensure that as many as possible get the message.

I suppose you could liken this to an advertising leaflet drop – chasing round to advertise yourself or a company as the biggest and best in your field. The point is that you are working, and not going out for pleasure.

Show your dog this is not a job that needs to be done – if it pulls towards a marking post, wall, gate or other suitable point, do not let him dictate your movement. For a start, your dog's controlling your movement and therefore in charge; and second, it's doing the unnecessary work of leaving messages, advertising its presence – the big boy on the block.

All you have to do is simply and silently guide the dog away by changing direction. When it is at your side, offer praise, maybe offer a food reward initially, and carry on your way. You've made nothing of what it was intending to do and shown your dog it is not necessary. You're taking the dog for a walk and not a boundary-marking session.

Bitches also mark like this – and the solution is the same.

I would also discourage excessive sniffing. With aggressive dogs, you are saying, 'Don't dwell on the fact that a fully mature male was here half an hour ago…let's go and have fun.' Standing around will only zone the dog on to smells that you would like to show it are of no consequence. Sniffing is good, but pick your spots; I'd rather they sniff the roses than boundary check.

Attacking the Vacuum Cleaner

First, remember that your dog doesn't understand what this strange, growling, backwards-and-forwards-moving beast is for, and it never will. Ensure your dog is relaxed before you start anything and you will get a far better response.

- Why not just have it out in the room as a new ornament, so the dog gets used to it just sitting there? Walk past it every now and again and touch it.

- In a day or so, walk past and turn it on and off and walk away, making absolutely nothing of it. The slower you do all this, the better.

- When you do vacuum, start off in the furthest part of the house away from the dog. If you live in a very small space and this is not practical or possible, then *never push the appliance towards the dog*. Focus instead on having your back view facing the dog.

- It may be better, particularly if your dog gets very upset by these things, to be separated by a baby gate initially and, when the dog reacts, then simply stop and shut the solid door until it is calm, then begin again.

With a lot of these problems, it is a great idea to start sorting these extra issues out when you have had a week or two of getting to grips with the five basic principles of PURE Dog Listening (p. 25). This gives your dog time to understand where you are coming from and build trust in you and your decisions.

Do make sure there is an escape route for the dog, so if it simply wishes to take itself off to another room while you're doing the housework, then it can. There should be no pressure on the dog to watch and learn – you're never going to expect him to do the housework. Or the gardening, for that matter, as it's worth remembering that, in a dog's mind, the lawnmower is an outside vacuum cleaner.

Avoiding Play

If you can't relax then usually you won't be able to play and enjoy yourself. Dogs are great play animals – they learn through play – but if you're the one with responsibilities above your capabilities or completely perplexed by life and wish the world would stop, then play will be last on your agenda.

So take the responsibility and confusion away and then your dog will relax and you'll be able to teach it that play is fun wherever you are. Some dogs will play in the garden but not out and about; they are relaxed in the garden or house and struggle out of their safe zone. Take responsibility away from them and find the lovely, happy dog in there that you never knew existed.

'Follow Me' is a great start – run and have fun. Loosen up.

Tail Chasing

This is another behaviour a dog does when it is in a pickle and doesn't know what to do. It may have done it as a pup and everyone roared with laughter; it got a reaction and a positive one at that, and it is just repeating the behaviour.

In many instances, it becomes an obsessive behaviour and is

simply put right by taking the dog by the collar and holding it until it relaxes – no speech, eye contact or emotion as always when correcting unwanted behaviour. You then step away and repeat the procedure as necessary, with no eye contact and no vocals. Persevere – you may not solve this overnight but you'll be pleasantly surprised how quickly you'll see results.

Obsessive Light and Shadow Chasing

As with all obsessions, do not compound the issue by laughing and engaging your dog; this is how it all started in the first place. Watches reflecting on walls, sunlight on the kitchen cabinets... they can prove all too interesting. If you make something of it, it will become something to the dog. They don't understand what it is and just because you've highlighted it in the past, the dog thinks that it *is* of interest or maybe an issue that needs its attention. Some may just try to catch it, some are rather more upset about it and will bark at it, but if it is a problem then it needs to be sorted out as soon as possible.

To stop this behaviour, simply guide the dog away from the area of light without a word, maybe even take it into another room to divert the attention. If necessary, do this a few times and either distract by changing rooms and doing something else or, if the dog is really fired up, then put it in the Calm Walk (p. 59) away from the trigger. Then you can Calm Hold (p. 57) and relax.

Digging up the Garden

How strange it is that we humans will allow some species their natural behaviour but not others. People who have rabbits and chickens don't give it another thought when they dig holes because that's what they do, and we can often ignore a cat who prepares a hole to defecate in. A dog, well, that's another matter. The fact is that it's just being a dog, just as the cat, chicken and rabbit are just being themselves, too.

We never make a big deal of it with the other animals but we do with the dog as the hole is probably bigger.

The other reason, of course, is that we expect the dog to abide by our human rules and mind-read, and we do so love telling our dogs what to do. Here's a thought to hang on to: instead of talking at your dog... try listening. Dog Listening. Keep it PURE and you'll be amazed what you'll hear.

Your plants and plant pots may well be your pride and joy come the spring and summer. Then you get a dog who has designs on being the next Alan Titchmarsh in the family. Its fingers are not green and the only redesigning it has done has turned the garden into your worst nightmare. Under these circumstances, the following suggestions will help:

- Do not make a big drama out of it, because if you do the dog will have got your attention and will very likely do it bigger and better next time.

- However mad you feel, just take your dog by the collar and lead it away. Calm Walk (p. 59), release the dog on the line away from the disaster area, then clear up the mess.

- If your dog decides that it is going to turn this into a game of chase, then back off and begin clearing up the pots (whether inside your house or outside), completely blanking it.

- Next time the dog is in the garden, make sure you have a long line attached to his collar so you can take hold of it.

- If the dog makes a beeline for your begonias, reel it in and hold it for a minute or two in silence. Then release. Step away and, when it is busy pottering or looking to go back to your plants, then recall it to you and reward.

- Show your dog it is getting nothing for the destruction and everything for the good stuff. Do not leave your dog unattended in the garden if it has a long line on or indeed if it has a tendency to do the gardening. A time will come when you can trust it to behave.

- Alternatively, show your dog a place in your garden where it can dig – and let it be a dog.

With a young puppy who hasn't got into the pattern of obsessive digging yet, you could just do a simple recall and take it off to do something else. Either way, it has not got any attention for what it has just been doing. Maybe give it a sandpit of its own.

Cuddles

Not all dogs like cuddles and strokes, especially from strangers. As mentioned already, we all love a good massage but we're certainly not going to get a complete stranger to do it.

Dogs have their own personalities, likes and dislikes. Just because it's a dog and has fur doesn't mean it likes any Tom, Dick or Harry in close proximity. Be thoughtful and watch the body language. You often see presenters on TV with unfamiliar dogs and it's surprising that more are not bitten: faces too close, trying to kiss and cuddle dogs they don't know. You can see fear in the dog's eyes, and fear in their stance but, bless them, most put up with us getting over-friendly fortunately.

Some people say their dog doesn't do cuddles. It's the same reason dogs don't play or relax – too stressed, too busy. When they can relax because you have given them good reason to by taking stress away from them, then you'll find a cuddly dog inside breaking out for love and attention on your terms.

Fussy Eaters

In my view, there is no such thing as a fussy eater. We make them so. Yes, there are some dogs that like particular foods, and prefer just to stick with it. Give them a variety if you like by adding left-over vegetables and meat (with no added salt).

Dogs are opportunists and hunters. There is a kind of dog that will manipulate you into feeding it when and what it wants – one week it will eat the supermarket special and stop the next week, so you try a deluxe brand. It eats that for a week and then stops and looks lovingly at your steak and chips. If the dog gets some, then you're on that slippery slope.

You've made a rod for your own back and the dog's got you where it wants you – trained. I had a client who would drive to the very expensive delicatessen in the village every morning and buy a selection of cold meats for his dog to make his daily choice. The following day, the process was repeated.

Within a week of the consultation, the dog was eating what he was given and the wine list was a thing of the past. The dog was a lot happier in himself, looked healthier and life was a lot more pleasant for my client when he cleared the garden. When a dog hunts in the wild, his preferred prey is not chorizo, salami or black pudding!

Some dogs can't eat in the morning as they are so anxious about what is to confront them during the day. Then, with some dogs, there are times that they lose their appetite every now and again due to something that has happened or changed within the dynamics of their family. Whatever the reason, this behavioural problem is very straightforward to correct.

If you're relaxed, you can eat, and if you're not trying to prove a point and take control, you can eat. There are five main times during a dog's day that tells it whether it is the main decision-maker or not. One of these is who controls feeding times. Take a look at the feeding chapter (p. 28) to get this right. Also be aware that if this behaviour has just kicked in, your dog may be feeling unwell and/or have a problem with its mouth or teeth, so get it checked out.

Dogs are not grazers and should not be left in control of a bowl of food throughout the day. It gives them ideas above their station.

If your dog generally eats well, but has suddenly gone off its food for no apparent reason, then this may well be an indication it is unwell. Please get it checked by your vet.

Noise Anxiety

Whether your dog is bothered by Bonfire Night depends to some extent on its personality but mostly on your skills as a decision-maker, showing your dog that whatever it is frightened of you're there for it, and your dog can relax with you and know all is well. So what you do when your dog freaks out on 5 November is more important than what the dog does.

When we are scared we often feel better if someone puts a reas-suring arm around our shoulders or offers a few soothing words. But dogs are not humans and to offer your dog a cuddle and to talk reas-suringly to it when it is in an anxious state will make the situation worse. You are giving it attention for this behaviour and therefore reinforcing the fear.

The key thing to remember is not to engage with your dog when it is stressed. This may be initially very difficult for many dog owners but it becomes second nature with a little practice. If the dog runs into a corner shaking, don't react. If the dog comes to you, just hold the dog still in a Calm Hold (p. 57). Take hold of its collar and draw it close to you, gently placing the palm of your hand over its shoul-ders, making gentle contact and wait for it to relax, not stroking it or engaging it in any way. Draw your dog close and sit back on the sofa with your legs resting on the dog's side. You are relaxed and your dog will come to understand that you are calm and unfazed. If you're not worried then your dog needn't be either. If you've ever been with someone who has just lost a loved one or experienced some other traumatic event, simply placing your hand on theirs and saying nothing is the best thing you can do. You are saying silently that you are there. As Ronan Keating put it: 'You say it best when you say nothing at all.'

It is not merely the noise of thunder that the dog will react to – it will become agitated long before the storm hits. The atmosphere is different. Some humans get headaches prior to a storm, so try to exude calmness.

Some dogs don't react to storms but do to fireworks. Maybe they had a bad experience or maybe not, but it is scary, with high-pitched whizzes and bangs. They can be deafening for an animal with such sensitive hearing.

Living with Other Dogs and Cats

Generally, if a dog is brought in as a puppy then there is little problem integrating the two; it's rescues that I've found to be more problematic. With a puppy, again do not make a fuss if it dashes up to a cat at home; the cat will find a bolt-hole. Do, however, guide your pup away and make nothing of the episode – it is only being inquisitive.

If these animals are to get on well together at home then we need to think about some key points. For example, wherever possible, provide a bolt-hole for the cat. It can be upstairs or in a particular room which is a no-go area for the dog. The 'off limits' status of this area can be reinforced by the use of a baby gate if required. Feed the cat in its safe area to relieve stress – a dog will always go for the cat's food because it's often left down longer than their own food. The dog can, by eating it, enhance its status. Don't give it the chance.

To teach the animals to co-exist calmly at least, implement the following strategy. You will need two people; your assistant should wait outside or in another room with your dog.

- Have your cat in the same room as you. If possible, have the cat on your lap stroking it but not facing the door where the dog comes in. Do not freak the cat out by holding him so he is scared rigid. Let him run if he wants to, but have another exit for him.

- Your assistant does a short stint of 'Follow Me' by using the technique of random changes in both pace and direction, interspersed with unsignalled halts, outside the room. This is really to focus the dog and remind it to pay attention to the humans and not to anything else.

- Your assistant should enter the room with the dog on a lead. If the dog as much as looks at the cat, then immediately walk out of the room with the dog.

- Repeat until the dog comes into room and lies down (still on the lead), ignoring the cat. Then allow the cat to move.

- If the dog reacts to the cat's movement, then walk out with your dog and start again until the lesson is learnt.

- As with all these techniques, don't rush. It takes as long as it takes. Keep calm and act like a leader, making the point that you will not accept bad behaviour. As the decision-maker, *you* decide who can be a family member. Remember that although you can teach a dog that any cat that you bring into your home is a member of your family, most dogs will still consider strange cats as fair game.

Bottom Shuffling

We've all seen dogs do this, dragging their backsides across the floor as if taking part in the Winter Olympics only to find out that someone's stolen their toboggan. This is a common problem with an easy solution. Your dog probably has impacted anal glands and they need emptying. A quick trip to a vet will soon sort it out. You could even do it yourself at home, if you are adventurous and there happens to be nothing on television. I'd hazard a guess that if you try it once then the next time the procedure is needed you'll be down the vet's as quickly as you can. Does it smell? Yes. Perhaps I should clarify that by saying, 'Yes... it *really* smells!' Does the dog mind? Once the glands are emptied, the dog feels great relief but the process can annoy or cause them discomfort. It's hardly dignified – would you stand calmly discussing the weather while your back passage was being squeezed and probed?

Bottom shuffling could also be an indication that your dog has worms of some variety, so do ensure that it is regularly treated.

Eating Faeces

There are many theories relating to coprophagia – it can be fear-based, either to hide the fact from humans that they've defecated because they have been reprimanded for it in the past, or it could be an attempt to hide their presence from other dogs. If a dog is eating its own waste, it is said that adding certain items to the food such as pineapple or courgettes makes the faeces unpalatable. As though it was tasty beforehand! It should go without saying that you add the pineapple or other chosen extra to the dog's food prior to feeding. It has been known for some owners who have been advised to try this method, rather than adding to the food, they have kept their dog under observation and then, as soon as their dog has defecated, they have rushed out and placed a piece of pineapple on top of the still steaming mound like a cherry on top of a trifle. This variation on a theme is very colourful but generally does not work.

It could be, too, that the dog is not getting all it needs from its present food, particularly if at a stage of rapid growth. As a guide to how a dog is managing with its food, ask yourself, 'Does it look healthy? Is it growing at the correct rate? Are its faeces firm and not foul-smelling?' If you are unsure, get the dog checked by a vet.

If you decide to change your dog's food, do it gradually so that it doesn't get 'food A' one day and 'food B' the next. Before going to the hassle of a complete diet change, try adding a pot of natural yogurt to your dog's food to increase the natural bacteria in the gut which may have been stripped out by loose stools or a dose of anti-biotics. The bacteria improve the digestion and absorption of all the nutrients from the food. You can always ask your vet for advice and weigh your dog at the clinic.

If the dog eats its faeces, clear it up promptly after you have called your dog to you. If it eats other dogs', then make sure you have great recall (p. 97) and great treats for when it returns. Engage with your dog on walks so it doesn't get distracted.

Mounting

When your dog decides to display mounting – more commonly called 'humping' – behaviour, it throws us humans into a state of embarrassment and confusion. 'Why does he do that?' we ask. The answer is simple . . . because he's a dog and that is what dogs do. They don't have our sensibilities. They exhibit behaviour, any behaviour, because that seems to be the right thing to do at that time. Both dogs and bitches will mount; it matters not whether they are entire or neutered. They'll do it to other dogs of the same or opposite sex. They'll do it to their beds, cuddly toys or your favourite cushions and, of course, worst of all, to humans.

Most dog owners who are subjected to these displays by their dogs tell us that it occurs far more frequently when they have guests, particularly when they're trying to make a good impression. The vicar comes to tea or the boss comes to dinner and there is a possible promotion in the offing when, game on, the dog starts performing. We don't know how to deal with it so we often make a joke of it or get angry and shout at the dog. We can get embarrassed and pretend it's not happening. Sometimes, the recipient of the dog's attentions even tries casually to walk away. Not so fast! The dog remains clamped to the leg as it is dragged across the room in a caricature of a Torvill and Dean ice dance routine.

So why is the dog causing such upset among the humans witnessing his amorous approaches to the vicar? He's attention-seeking or just in a pickle. What the dog is saying to its audience is, 'Hey everybody! Look over here! Great – you've stopped talking to the vicar and now you're talking to me, I'm therefore even more important than usual and I'm learning how to get your attention. This owner-training is really easy!'

This behaviour also is displayed by a lot of dogs when dynamics change in the room and they get anxious. Not quite sure what to do with themselves, as in tail chasing, they will mount their doggy pal or cushion.

Once again, it's just a matter of seeing what the dog sees in every situation and then we can resolve it. Simply hold your dog away by the collar and wait for it to settle, and repeat as necessary. Again, do not engage in any eye contact or talking as this is perceived as encouragement and reward.

Castration often won't help, in my opinion, as the problem is generally in the head rather than the nether regions, unless, of course, a bitch is coming into season or is in season. There may well be a possibility of too much testosterone, but rather than castrate and find it doesn't work, try correcting the behaviour first.

If castration has been suggested for a behavioural problem, why not chemically castrate first to see whether it is beneficial? At least with this method, if it makes the situation worse, whether humping or aggression, it can be reversed. Once surgically castrated, always castrated.

Castration is often seen by humans as the panacea for all ills – it isn't, and early castration before the dog is fully mature, both in body and mind, can cause more problems than the ones you hope to address through the procedure. In some cases, it won't solve the original problem anyway.

As pups mature, at about six to eight months, their testosterone level rises much higher than an adult and this can result in such behaviour. As they get to adulthood it drops to within normal levels, so don't rush for castration. Deal with it as above. It can start off as a teenage thing and become an attention-seeking display if you do not deal with it thoughtfully.

11

Rescue Dogs

I have three rescue dogs and they all came with their particular issues. All are a delight in their own special way and what they have taught me more than anything is that patience and kindness pays off. I also work with a rescue centre in Dorset, to help ensure their behavioural issues are addressed at the centre so they may find their lifelong homes.

Some dogs have been mistreated or are just plain confused. Some have had many homes, some maybe only one. In all cases, they have been placed in a refuge for a variety of reasons. Many of these dogs were bought as fluffy little bundles of fun at about eight weeks of age. As a dog matures, it begins to need more food, more exercise and more of the owner's time. It also may have presented with behavioural problems that are unacceptable to their owners who find certain issues unworkable.

Some dogs have lost the ability to communicate with their own, or refuse and are unable to communicate with humans, as they may have been punished for doing what dogs do, or never had a loving human touch. This is where we may come across dogs that are introvert, withdrawn, closed off or completely off the wall.

Re-homing these vulnerable dogs is not always easy, as people often perceive older dogs to be untrainable – but this is not the case. Remember, you *can* 'teach an old dog new tricks'. So bear in mind, if you do take on a rescue dog, it may well need more time to gain that trust. Don't focus on its past – you may never know it, anyway – but make allowances for nervousness by being compassionate, calm and patient.

All dogs deserve to be understood. Whenever I am called to see such a dog with behavioural problems, a line is drawn on that day – what is past is past. Knowing the past is very helpful, but if this is not forthcoming then we deal with the behaviour issues it presents and focus on the future. Work with your new friend and show the dog that it is safe and secure in its new home. It's a feeling all canines deserve, and which we should provide.

Taking Your Rescue Dog Home

Eye Contact
In the dog world, eye contact is a means of communication, so don't keep looking at your dog or it will make it feel uncomfortable as canines don't meet face on and it may seem confrontational. Your dog will also think that you want it to do something for you, so it won't be able to relax. Don't look at your dog all the time – give it a break.

Calm in the Car
Place the dog in a secure place in the car and drive home. This is not the time to reassure, as the dog will feel that you are worried, too. By all means, put your hand on its back for reassurance (no tickling)

– this is a good, calm connection as it can feel your lowered pulse rate.

Toileting Area

Take the dog straight to the place where you want it to relieve itself. Give it time and space to perform and praise if it does.

Sleeping and Drinking Place

Show the dog the kitchen and give it time to explore without making a fuss. Keep calm and give it time to adjust to its new surroundings. Don't give it the whole house to explore as it will be too overwhelming.

Slow and Gentle Adjustment

During the first few days, try to disregard the dog as much as you can. Give it time to adjust to its new surroundings without putting pressure on it to perform. Call it to make a fuss of it and give a treat, but don't nag. In this case, less is most definitely more.

First Few Nights

If you want to (it's not compulsory), it is perfectly all right to allow your dog to sleep by your bed on the first night. This will probably reassure both of you. It is then a simple matter of moving the dog to your bedroom doorway, to the top of the stairs, then the bottom of the stairs and then the desired sleeping place over the next week or two.

Find an old, unwashed T-shirt or sweater and put it in the dog's bed. This will give the dog the reassurance of the scent of the new family.

First Two Weeks

There is no rush to take your dog out to explore all the places you walk, or go to all the places you want to visit. It may never have seen more than a back yard before. So take it slowly, introduce the dog to things gradually over the first couple of weeks. Why not let it just potter about the home and garden getting to know you and its new home? Your time would be best spent getting the dog to trust you with the methods in this book.

You'll not be presented with all behaviour problems for at least the first eight weeks. Dogs are so different when they get their feet under the table and become relaxed; then you will see what you've got. So just because your new arrival is quiet and good, things may well change.

Your new friend needs time to adjust, to take the pressure off – it may well just want to sleep. Teach it to come when called, in the home and garden, and show it the kind, human touch. Be patient and give your dog time to adjust.

If the dog has been in a foster home, they will have taken the dog out and know whether it is good on the lead, chases cats, great with children, is not frightened of cars and doesn't bark at bikes. Good rescue centres will have assessed the dog for a couple of weeks, made sure it is healthy and assessed the dog's behaviour well.

All rescue centres will want to check you out, so make sure you check them out, too, ensuring that you will get ongoing help and advice if you need it.

Non-communicative Dogs

Every now and again I come across dogs that have been severely affected by their past. Some will become shut down, unresponsive and withdrawn. In my experience, this is often due to:

- Being in a very large group of dogs and bullied into keeping out of the way, creating the belief that trouble will be avoided if the dog keeps its head down.

- Having had no human contact, or being in a home where the dog has been completely overwhelmed.

- Being punished for being a dog and doing doggy things.

- Having no other dog or human contact.

These guys need even more time and patience; they need to get used to things going on around them and no pressure of performing even a recall. They need time to mend and listen and watch.

I'd start off by just priority feeding and, rather than a bowl of food in an open kitchen, I'd place a large piece of chicken very close so they can nip out and take it back to their bed to eat in safety.

The chicken is a tasty morsel to tempt a dog which refuses to eat because it is too fearful to emerge from its bolt-hole. It is not a lure to promote contact. So leave the room at first after depositing, then, when it starts to come out, stand in the doorway, but face away, gradually working round to being in the same room as the feeding dog – and take it from there.

In the wild, if the dog had made a small kill or scavenge then the product would be taken to a safe place by the dog. In the same way it wouldn't sleep out in a wide open space unprotected by camouflage or friends.

I would also make a point of walking through the room or being in the room where the dog's bolt-hole is – not making contact – but showing the dog that you have the right to be in that space.

Make sure your dog has a place to sleep away from the thorough-fare of house traffic; a corner in the kitchen is a great place. A crate is ideal with a blanket over the top and sides, or a bed placed under a table. Make this bed space a no-go area for all except your dog. Also ensure it is not facing the door, so people don't automatically stare at the dog on entry.

Do not expect too much too soon; these dogs have a huge amount of baggage to unload and it will take many months, not weeks, to mend them. And don't be tempted to smother them with cuddles and love; it may make you feel better, but the dog may well not appreciate it. If the dog comes to you when called, then gently stroke it with little eye contact.

They have to relax at home and start to enjoy life with no pressure, learn to play and eat in comfort and safety. If your new dog has never been in a house before, then it is going to be extremely stressful for it with all the new noises and smells. These dogs are generally best placed in homes where they do have great outside space to enjoy with their new human friends.

12

Children and Dogs

Every child should have a pet, preferably a dog, but then I'm biased. Pets – and dogs in particular – teach children so many things: to care for another creature in an unselfish way; loyalty; and even the facts of life… and death. All this helps to make children better able to interact not only with animals but also with fellow humans and allows them to grow into well-balanced and caring adults.

If you decide to bring a dog into your household with your children, it is important that both dog and children have guidelines. It is advisable to teach the children how to interact with the new addition to the family before it arrives and gets swamped by over-excited playmates.

The following tips may prove useful and should be highlighted to children at home:

- Treat a dog as you would like to be treated – don't pull its ears or tail. Never shout at it – the dog won't forget how you treat it.

- Even if it looks kind, don't approach your dog. If it wants to come to you, it will.

- Avoid things that might threaten the dog; for example, backing it in a corner, running at it, shouting at it.

- Never look at the dog in the eyes – it may be taken as an invitation to fight.

- Don't go near his tail, don't pull it or step on it. It is used to express feelings.

- Don't disturb a dog when it's eating and never try to take its food away – it'll defend it instinctively.

- When you play with it, don't pet it near its teeth. The dog likes catching things and it could be your fingers.

- Never try to separate fighting dogs; go and get help from an adult you know.

- Whether you are afraid or not, never run away from a dog as it'll take it as an invitation to chase you.

- You have two hands – your dog has only its teeth to hold on to you. Often you may think it wants to bite, but it may only want to hold on to you.

- Only play with a dog when you are with an adult – dogs respect them more because they are larger.

- Never play tug of war. It can get out of hand very easily with the wrong personality of dog.

- No two dogs are the same; you have to get to know them. Treat them kindly and gently and gain their respect.

- If you are expecting a few children into the house, then put the dog in a safe place. If the children are getting over-excited with the new addition, give them breathing space apart. Your four-legged friend will thank you for it.

Babies and Dogs

I receive a number of enquiries from concerned dog owners because they are either expecting or have just had a baby. Quite often a 'well-meaning' friend will put the fear of God into the parents with tales of 'killer dogs' and they will be advised to re-home or even destroy their family dog. 'The dog will be jealous...' they are told.

The truth is: give the right information to dog and child and there will be no problem. The bond between children and dogs is wonderful to see.

To illustrate just how baby-orientated and nurturing a dog can be, one client had suffered several miscarriages and had almost given up on ever being a mother. One day, she fed her dog and settled down in front of the TV. Her dog came into the lounge and regurgitated its meal in her lap. The following day, this lady was at her doctor's to announce that she was pregnant. (I'm not sure whether that would have been my first reaction unless I wanted to be sectioned!) When asked the usual questions about dates, symptoms and so on, she told the GP that her dog had told her by its actions the previous evening.

You can just imagine the doctor inching away, keeping the desk between them and saying, 'Yes, I see... I'm just going to stand over here now.' However, she was right and now has a very healthy boy.

The amazing thing about this is that during the previous pregnancies their dog had never exhibited this behaviour although the pregnancies had been confirmed and a due date given. Did the dog somehow know that these pregnancies were not viable? I don't know for certain, but canines will bring back food from the hunt and regurgitate it for a nursing mother. OK, this lady wasn't a nursing mother, and it is an extreme reaction and may well have been a coincidence, but we always have to remember that dogs have what we like to call the sixth sense. Generally, dogs will become clingy to a pregnant lady rather than vomit on them! They are so in tune with our and their bodies that the slightest chemical changes are painfully obvious to them. This is why we now have medical detection dogs being trained to notify their owners of imminent medical issues like diabetic crisis and epileptic fits.

So, you've got your new baby and you bring it home. There will be all sorts of excitement and strange new sights, sounds and smells for your dog to get used to. You will be exhausted and pleased to be home. Don't get into a situation where you are trying to get through the door with new baby and all the equipment that entails, as well as relatives, friends and neighbours all trying to welcome the new arrival, with a dog bouncing around trying to get noticed, too.

Keep the dog in another room – a happy room, such as where it normally sleeps or maybe the kitchen. Most dogs like kitchens as it's the hub of the house and the food connection makes it a good place to be. A family member can go into the kitchen to make tea or coffee and interact with the dog as usually happens on other days. This shows that the status quo is unchanged; the pack still has credible leaders. It's vital that the dog doesn't feel isolated as it's done nothing wrong.

Everything is done on your terms, so in your own time settle down comfortably with the baby so that you are relaxed and confident in your own comfort zone. Your partner or a friend can now bring your dog into the room on the lead without any stress being imposed on dog or humans. Chat among yourselves – there may well be other people in the room – and make sure these people disregard the dog and only interact with one another. As always, keep calm, but if your dog is unsure of what is going on and therefore unsettled, then remove it from the room without any drama. Allow it time to realise that everybody is relaxed and then bring it back into the room. This takes as long as it takes, proceeding at your own pace. The person holding the dog can then sit near the parent holding the baby and chat. Don't rush – we humans can become obsessed with schedules and timetables so that we can tick a box as 'job done'.

Dogs, though, don't have watches – to a dog, the time is always 'now'. Because you are relaxed, your dog will also feel at peace. When the dog decides to investigate the new arrival, it will do this by both looking and sniffing. Keep calm and allow it to sniff around the feet but don't allow access to the head and face. At this early stage, your baby probably won't appreciate a large, wet tongue moving across its face!

All newborn animals are vulnerable and reliant on their parents for survival. Nature gives them a tool to ensure that Mum and Dad are kept aware of their existence. It is the cry, that ear-piercing, head-splitting wail that says, 'Give me attention...NOW!' You, as the parent, have to interpret that sound and decide whether your child is hungry, in pain, needs a nappy change or just wants attention.

This explosion of noise may well disturb your dog the first few times it hears it, but if you deal with the baby calmly it will see that you have everything under control, that you are a strong, credible leader. If you go into headless chicken mode, you give a very different message to the dog – i.e. that you can't cope. If you can't cope, it means that your dog will have to, but it won't be able to cope either. A downward spiral...panic all round. Although you must remain calm, of course you must also remain vigilant, so never leave a baby or young child alone with any dog.

Children sometimes are not taught that dogs, cats or, indeed, all animals are sentient beings and should be treated with respect. They are not there to be pulled around or ridden. Sadly, some parents think it is something to boast about that their child 'can do anything' with the dog. Teach your child to respect all animals – it is your responsibility as parents and it will make your child a better human being, too.

13

Puppies

Choosing and Bringing a Puppy Home

My preferred option when considering ownership of a new dog is always to think about rescues first. But there's no denying it – it's lovely to have a new puppy.

Here is some advice to help you find the right one and then introduce it happily into your home:

- Buy from reputable breeders who limit themselves to one breed and the number of litters they deal with.

- An advert where any more than one breed is listed as 'available' should ring alarm bells.

- Don't deal with anyone who only gives a mobile phone number as their contact details.

- Don't buy from a breeder who wants to deliver the puppy to you rather than ask you to collect. Some of these breeders will even want you to meet them in a motorway service area for the exchange. This is a real, living, feeling creature we are dealing with, not actors in a B-movie spy story.

- Make sure the breeder will take back puppies for whatever reason at whatever age to re-home. These are the breeders who really care about the pups they produce.

- If you cannot see the mother, then leave. If the mother or pups look unwell or under-nourished, leave. If at any stage you get a bad feeling about the place, leave. It is only this that will stop unscrupulous breeding. It is hard not to feel sorry for the pups and think, 'I'll take one or two on just to get them out of there.' The kindest thing to do is to report the breeder to The Kennel Club and RSPCA. That will help stop puppy farming. Don't be duped by the breeder saying the bitch looks skinny because she is feeding lots of pups... she is simply not getting fed enough to keep up with demand.

- Make sure you see proof the puppies have been vet checked.

- You should not take a puppy away from its litter and mother before eight weeks of age. If the breeder is insisting, then walk away. Between six and eight weeks the puppy learns a huge amount from its littermates and mother – how hard to bite, what it can get away with and other vital lessons. It learns some manners from its mother and learns how to interact with its siblings, which is a learning curve not to be missed. Miss this out and you may well be setting yourself up for trouble and end up owning a puppy with fewer skills in how to interact with its own kind.

- Take your time choosing a puppy from the right litter; don't fall for the first pup in the first litter you see.

- Make sure it has been brought up in a house with all the usual comings and goings and noises and smells. Proper socialisation at this age is so important for a well-adjusted puppy and makes moving to a new home less stressful. If you have children, it is ideal to obtain your puppy from someone who has had well-behaved children round the puppies during these formative weeks.

- Prepare all you will need for your puppy before it arrives – bowls, bed, etc.

- When your puppy arrives home for the first time, take it outside so it can relieve itself.

- Give it a meal, then let it investigate its new surroundings – a small area to begin with e.g. the kitchen.

- Be there with it, but put no pressure on it. Give it space and show your puppy right from the start that it is safe with you.

- Understand your puppy needs time and patience and understanding. It will test you but it is never naughty, it's just a young dog who needs guidance and set boundaries as it grows up.

- Take it for a 'once over' to your vet's at the end of the first week (if concerned, take it before) and discuss vaccinations and worming. Please read the section on castration (p. 156) and do some research yourself – there is loads of information both for and against on various websites. Make an informed decision.

- What do you do if a puppy jumps up at you? You guide it down and stroke it with all four feet on the ground.

- What do you do if your puppy of eight to sixteen weeks nips you? Short, sharp 'Ow!' and walk away, then try calling the pup to you and stroke. Don't wear floppy sleeves if you have a nippy puppy as it will only try to grab these as a game. Make it easy on you and the puppy.

- What do you do if the puppy has an accident on a carpet inside? Clear it up. Do not tell your puppy off, it is not the puppy's fault and remember to take it out more regularly – after meals, when they have woken up – and reward with praise and food when they perform in the correct place.

- What if your puppy follows you constantly? Remember to close doors behind you. Do not let the puppy follow you everywhere – to the toilet, etc. – as you will be creating a dog with separation anxiety as it matures to adulthood.

- It will also be helpful to read the guidelines on The Kennel Club website.

Having looked at what you should do to choose and integrate a puppy successfully, here's what you *shouldn't* do:

- Pick your puppy up if it looks ill – for example, with runny eyes, dry nose, runny nose, sore patches, fur missing, or signs of diarrhoea. Don't let your heart rule your head.

- Get all your friends and neighbours round to cuddle and meet it – your puppy needs to settle in and be comfortable in its new surroundings and get used to the family before meeting others.

- Take it out for a walk in the big wide world immediately after it's had its injections and let it run free – the puppy will get it all wrong, as a human toddler would if you didn't hold its hand.

- Tell the puppy off if it has an accident in the house. Instead, reward it when it performs correctly in the garden.

- Encourage rough games – it'll get it wrong. As the puppy grows, it will get out of hand and accidents will happen.

- Tell your puppy how to behave. Show it and get it thinking of its own free will.

- Do too much 'Sit', 'Stay' and 'Heel' – they are the icing on the cake to be taught without pressure. It's how your puppy responds to you in daily life that is important. Does it jump up? Does it bite you? Does it hang on your clothes? Does it follow you constantly and seem unable to rest? Show the puppy how to respect you – the only way to do this is by using its own language, the only one it truly understands completely.

- Remember, there is no rush to bombard your puppy with information about the outside world. Let it find its feet at home and go out slowly but surely when the pup is comfortable with you.

Crate Training

This is recognised as an important aspect of successful training as there are times when your dog will need to be crated, such as at the vet's; you might have a small house and would like to place the dog in a safe area when you have loads of visitors; or it may have need of confinement if it has had a medical procedure. Shutting the door for short periods during the day when the pup is asleep or you are out, and at night when it is very young, will mean that it sees this as a good place to be. It also has the added benefit of helping you to potty train it.

Feeding it in the crate will also help you show the pup it is a lovely place to be.

Puppy Socialisation

Birth to Eight Weeks

This is the most important period in a dog's life. Get this right and you'll have a well-adjusted puppy leaving for its new home. So whether you are looking for a puppy or you have a litter, by reading this you should have a good idea of what to do as a breeder and what to look for as a new owner.

Roger Abrantes, the eminent author and expert in animal behaviour, has written: 'The very first stage of a puppy's life is called the "imprinting" stage. This is followed by a "socialisation" stage. If these stages are managed correctly, puppies have an excellent foundation to be a happy, well-adjusted and well-trained pet. If these stages are managed badly, puppies can display a whole range of problems.'

From his research, Abrantes has found that although a lot can be done to make improvements for these problem puppies, the damage can never be fully repaired.

Our suggestion is to pick puppies that have been brought up in the home environment learning about all the strange noises we make and the clatter-bangs of our various gadgets that we humans find hard to do without and that dogs can't make sense of at all. In the home, they get desensitised to the sounds of the vacuum cleaner, washing machine, comings and goings, and so on.

The imprinting period is from birth to eight weeks, so the breeder should spend a few minutes twice a day in the early stages holding and cooing at each pup individually, so they get used to the kind human touch and kind voice. Then as pups get bigger and the mum is happy, then these cuddles should be lengthened to about ten minutes twice or three times a day.

Only family members who live in the house should do this in the first four weeks or you're liable to upset the bitch and unsettle the pups. After four weeks, then others can be asked to do the same but do supervise adults and children. If the bitch is uneasy, then place her away at this stage, but if she is well brought up and social, then you should have no issues really. But remember they are her babies.

Never loom over the whelping box or pick a pup up by the scruff; the mother will hold a pup gently in her jaws and, when the weight is too much, she stops.

And move more slowly – a pup's eyesight is poor.

Handlers should be seated on the floor and cuddle the pup close to their chest and not dangle it in mid-air. I'd hate it, let alone a puppy who has just entered the world. We want them to trust and, like the human, not feel any anxiety.

Puppies should not be collected from the breeder before eight weeks of age. Some people will tell you that if you take them at seven weeks they will imprint on you better. This is entirely untrue. On the contrary, in fact – what you are doing is depriving your puppy of a week of vital learning with its mum and siblings. A week at this age with its mother and siblings is worth a pot of gold.

Eight Weeks to Six Months

When we get our puppy to its new home, we need to continue socialisation to people, children and animals. It doesn't mean we have to take it out to cocktail parties and school gates immediately. Short, quiet introductions are far more beneficial and less frightening. This period lasts up to about six months in age. Increase the experiences slowly but surely.

The first six months are the most important as puppies learn relationships for the rest of their lives, so get this right. If socialisation is not done correctly, then you will have a fearful dog with a whole host of issues. We can repair to a great extent, but why let your dog go through that stress?

When looking at puppy classes, make sure they are exactly what they say they are. Puppies up to sixteen weeks old are puppies. Older than this and mixing youngsters with adolescents can be problematic, especially if the adolescent has no bite inhibition and may have other issues that are being addressed.

Puppies need to be socialised within their own age group and the lessons need to be structured for them specifically, be fun and, hopefully, off-lead, too. A pup on a lead is going to get frustrated and bored. Too much lead work for an eight- to sixteen-week-old in a class environment, in my opinion, is too much pressure too soon.

It's my belief that puppies and dogs do not become aggressive because they have not had much contact with other dogs. They become aggressive generally through fear because they have been introduced to society under the wrong conditions, or perhaps have been put under too much pressure too soon to accept conditions that *we* perceive as non-threatening. Remember, aggression is not limited to dog-on-dog but can also relate to dog-on-human or dog-on-anything! These dogs do not have clear boundaries or feel they can trust the one they are with.

We see the same behaviour in children where parents either have no interest in their child, because it's too much effort and would interfere with their lifestyle or, at the other end of the spectrum, we have the parent who treats their child as a prince or princess and panders to their every whim. In both cases, it's not the child's fault but it makes it harder for them to interact with other members of society in a civilised manner.

So the important thing to remember is socialise with care and understanding; too much too soon can be frightening. Be choosy with your puppy's playmates. Work with puppies the same size as yours. If you have a Jack Russell then pick a Jack Russell-sized friend for it, not a socking great St Bernard. Let them play and work each other out but, if there is any sign of over-the-top play, then just calm things down by holding them calmly for a minute or two, then release. If they play too roughly, then accidents can happen.

Make sure the 'play space' is big enough so if one pup finds it too much it can get away and not feel penned in without any escape route. If it wants to hide, then let it. You can't force anyone to play; let them weigh up the situation and, when the time is right, they will. If there is a pup that goes over the top and is backing yours into a corner, then the big bumptious one should be led away quietly. We don't allow bullying, and it has to be shown that it is unacceptable. Your pup will be delighted.

Introduce your puppy to new places and things gradually. Getting bombarded by too much too soon can make an anxious pup more anxious and a boisterous one more so. As with everything, slowly but surely is the key. There is no rush – take your time and the puppy will take things in calmly at your side as you make decisions that enable it trust you.

Socialisation is not just between puppy and dogs or puppy and people, it is all that goes on around you. So be mindful of your environment. You will never be able to come across all you will encounter in your lives together in the first few months, so don't try to. You will overload the pup with too much information it's not yet ready to process. Get it to trust you and your actions and it'll be fine.

Guide your puppy through its young life into adulthood, gently showing it the rights and wrongs, so it may love you, trust you and live a stress-free life...a dog's life.

14

Good Health and Happiness

Grooming and Massage

Grooming and massage should be a daily occurrence, even if your dog has very short hair. It is a great way of spending prime relaxing time together. Get the dog used to this at a very early age then it won't become an issue for you or the dog.

With a puppy, it will initially try and turn it into a game, so you must resist this as it will only make things difficult in the future. So use a grooming glove or just your hands initially if a brush triggers the puppy into playing up; you can always use this method as well for an older dog who's having problems accepting grooming. Short and sweet, no pressure to do the whole body in one go.

Massage and groom every area, spending time even between the toes. This will ensure that when the dog goes to the vet's or have other types of grooming, it will more likely accept all the fiddling around by a stranger.

Begin by using the back of the brush so the puppy gets used to the feel of something alien on it. If the puppy tries to bite it, take the brush away and make no eye contact with the pup. This shows it that you are not interested in a game at this point and all you want to do is get a job done. As time goes by, the pup will enjoy this as some quality relaxing time with you, just like when you stroke your dog. It's great for the dog's blood pressure and yours.

If you have a long- or thick-haired dog, then the breeder should have given you advice on how to groom. If not, go to your local pooch parlour and ask them to teach you and watch them do it.

Apart from being a lovely thing to do, it gives you a great opportunity to feel any bumps or lumps your dog may have and be in a position to get them checked out at the first possible moment.

Castration

This issue has been mentioned already, in relation to aggression (p. 50) or mounting (p. 132) and possible solutions. There is a case to be made for castration. If you have both a dog and a bitch in your home, unless you intend to breed, you will either have to have at least one of them neutered or be very vigilant. If your vet advises you that your dog needs the procedure now to cure a medical problem, go ahead. If you do decide to go for the castration option, which many sensibly do, delay this if at all possible until the dog is at least fourteen months old. When a dog goes through puberty, it is not only testosterone that is pumped into the body but other vital chemicals which will be lost as a result of the procedure. These are all required for the growth and development of your dog into adulthood resulting in a healthy body and mind.

As humans, we can tell by pain or changes in our bodies that things aren't right and can visit our doctor. Dogs can't do this; they are by nature stoical creatures and don't want to show signs of weakness.

There is a train of thought that promotes keeping dogs entire until around age six and then, if there are no behavioural issues, considering castration to reduce the possibility of testicular cancer.

The usual advice given to deal with mounting behaviour and aggression is castration. It's my belief that castration will not generally cure aggressive behavioural problems; in many cases, it will not change anything and, in others, it makes them worse. If castration is the advice given, why not opt for chemical castration first to see if it has a positive effect on your dog's behaviour?

If you're a man, you'll know the answer to this next question. If you're a woman, ask your husband, partner or boyfriend whether he would be mellower and at peace with the world if you dragged him down to the local Health Centre one morning and had him 'modified'. Food for thought?

If considering the procedure, research it thoroughly and talk to your vet (because you will have chosen one you trust). Listen to professional advice, weigh up the pros and cons and then make an informed decision.

Spaying

When considering spaying a bitch, many of the same issues as castration arise in deciding whether to say 'yes' or 'no'. There is the possibility of unwanted pregnancy, the considerable mess that bitches can make when in season which embarrasses some owners, not forgetting, of course, the legions of male admirers that will be banging on your front door twenty-four hours a day at these times.

As with all dogs, the most important issue is disease prevention. It is wise if you are not going to breed to spay your bitch three months after her first season. If not done, then it would be a good decision to have a bitch spayed once she reaches six years as they have a tendency to get pyometra (an infection of the uterus) in later years.

It has been known, though, for bitches younger than this to contract this problem, so talk to your vet. Dogs live longer in domestic circumstances than they would in the wild, and throughout their lives they can collect benign cysts which later in life can become infected. If pyometra results, it is generally too late to save them as blood poisoning sets in.

As with all health concerns, know your dog, watch your dog. Is it drinking more or less than usual? Is it in pain or discomfort? Are its feeding or toilet behaviours different? If at all concerned, contact your vet with as much information as you can. Listen to your vet and make a decision.

15

To Breed or Not to Breed?

I am asked 'Would it be a good idea to breed?' many times, and I always answer with a question: 'Why do you want to do it?' and advise: 'Look into it very carefully before you go ahead.'

As a general rule of thumb, there are more than enough dogs out there and there is a massive problem with the number of rescue dogs coming in on a daily basis, without adding to the issue.

But if you are thinking of breeding, then you should look to the personality of your dog or bitch before embarking on breeding, as well as its physical health. An over-anxious or aggressive parent will produce a higher percentage of pups that are similar in personality. There are so many problems out there with dogs nowadays, and if only people who breed took personality more into consideration, then we wouldn't have half the issues we do today. So many dogs are either re-homed or put to sleep because of behavioural issues (which usually strike bigger and better at about eighteen to twenty-four months as they reach maturity). OK, most behavioural issues exist because there is a communication issue, but the tendency for extreme behaviours has to lie also with the breeding.

If you do breed, then do expect some comeback and consider having to allocate time to people asking for advice later on down the line...can you give this?

There are a number of points to consider. First, it is a myth that having a litter calms a bitch down. Some may, but it is not a guarantee. I've known bitches that have become aggressive through bad management by the breeder. Some bitches form the idea that because they have bred, it puts them higher up in the pecking order and they can become a problem thereafter.

Second, breeding is not a quick fix to pay off the bills! Sometimes a bitch will only have a couple of puppies, and if she needs a Caesarean that's the price of one pup gone already, and setting up to have pups with the right equipment is an expense in itself. The bitch will require double the amount of food during pregnancy and even triple her usual amount after whelping. Vet checks, vitamins and extra calcium all mount up.

It is hard work if you do it properly and then there is no guarantee that you will sell all the pups, so be aware that you may have to hold on to one or two.

You should also be in the position to take puppies back for whatever reason and at whatever age and either keep or be able to re-home puppies yourself.

I reckon it costs the price of three pups to have and rear a litter properly, maybe more if there are complications. When I've interviewed potential owners, a few have been turned away just on the phone. The main reason is if the partner is pregnant or they have a babe in arms. It's a big thing having a baby and just as exhausting having a puppy – we are not Wonder Women or Supermen! So give yourself a break, and get one sorted before you embark on the next

– you want it to work, so give yourself the best chance possible. I used to breed the odd litter, but have not for ten years now and never will again. There are too many dogs in need to add to the list.

No one wants to be a killjoy, but if you do decide to go ahead make sure you have the room, the time, the knowledge and the back-up. It is great fun to have lots of little bundles at home, but there is far more to it than that.

Do some research and go ahead with your eyes open.

16

More Than One Dog?

Are there two or more dogs in your family? Are you having to cope with multiple behavioural issues?

Invariably, those who have several dogs may have to deal with existing problems, or they are having problems introducing a new puppy or rescue dog to the gang.

What we have to remember is that if we sort out the relationship between the dogs and show them that they are all important as individuals, and try not to put one above the other just because it has either been with you longer or is older, we can smooth things out.

We have to, as we do with children and friends, give them their time, their moment and not feel that because one is getting attention that the other is in some way neglected. Sometimes you have to buy one child a new pair of shoes and not the other; it doesn't mean the other child won't get a pair when his shoes are too small or worn out!

Yes, of course, you can do things with your dogs together, but it is also essential that they see that sometimes it is just time for one. You can also liken it to helping one child with its homework or doing an activity and giving your all to them. There will be no jealousy if you give your time to each and every one of them. They, as with individual dogs, will get all they need and all they want, but in your time and your way.

There may be a 'Me, Me, Me' member in your group of dogs that always seems to get there first whether it be for a cuddle or the ball when playing. Manage the situation and the bully will realise that it can't wrap you round its paw, and the one who's in the background will become braver in the knowledge that you, the parent, will make sure all is fair.

When trying to deal with multiple dogs, the following guidelines will be worth remembering.

Treat Your Dogs as Individuals

Don't expect them to get it at the same time…they will in their own time. Each dog will have different issues and these have to be addressed with that individual. The number of times I am called to sort out a problem dog and the actual problem is in the pack.

Dynamics change, and when one dog no longer barks continually at the front door, then the other will take over as there is a job it feels needs filling. They work out their job specifications between them and, when one relinquishes, the other may feel it's now their job.

With any educational programme, we want the pupil to ask questions so they really understand and we know they understand the lesson. It is how we interpret these questions (many are extremely subtle) and answer these questions that is all important.

Don't become angered by questions – they are essential for learning. Just answer appropriately with no speech, no eye contact. It's what we do not say that plays a major part in getting the behaviour we desire from our dogs.

Call One, Hold the Other

We want each dog to learn that it is worthy in its own right and that it can come for a cuddle or groom without the other pushing it out of the way. You'll probably find when you call one dog over that they both come; this is fine, but not all the time, especially when you've only called one.

By holding the interloper to the side by its collar and saying nothing, it will learn to respect the other dog's space, your space and, above all, patience. Don't feel cruel, just remember when you ask one of your younger family members to sit on your lap, you don't expect to be crushed by everyone taking the liberty of doing the same! They will all get a piece of you when you decide and in your good time. Individual time and special one-to-one time is necessary for each and every one of us, including our dogs. It's not a case of anyone missing out.

Separate Training

You achieve nothing to begin with by trying to achieve walk training with both or all dogs at the same time. It is a game of 'Follow Me' and we need to get the individual lesson right first before we put them together.

When you have great 'Follow Me' individually, then start off together in the house and garden (if you have one), then move out slowly from the home as you did on an individual basis. You're showing them it is the same together as it is alone.

When you get them together initially, it may be a struggle as they will feed off each other and vie for the lead spot. Keep calm and you'll get there. No rush, it will happen with time, just have patience.

Separate Game-playing

You may well have one dog that always gets the ball so the other never plays with it. No surprise really, as each time it tried to go for a ball the other always got there first. So if this happens time and time again, then play will not be fun, so they don't bother.

Play separately to begin with; have valuable one-to-one time. Then as play gets very good, you can have the bully on a lead and throw for the other. The effect this will have is to show the bully you're not putting up with the butting in. Very importantly, it will also show the other dog that you're the one taking charge of proceedings and enable it to feel a little more assertive.

You may also need to accept that your dogs will have different levels of learning and attention. Be patient – one will respond to different activities and lessons better and quicker than the other. But they will catch up in the end.

There's no need to worry – they will both learn it all given the time and patience. Nothing worth having is easy.

The 15 Commandments

I   Thou shalt remember your dog can only be a dog.

II   Thou shalt remember – actions speak louder than words.

III   Thou shalt become fluent in canine for your dog to understand you.

IV   Thou shalt NOT treat your dog as a human.

V   Thou shalt reward good behaviour.

VI   Thou shalt be proactive with bad behaviour.

VII   Thou shalt understand your dog learns best when all is calm.

VIII   Thou shalt NOT use a command to correct a problem.

IX   Thou shalt walk with a loose lead.

X   Thou shalt NOT panic.

XI   Thou shalt remain calm and consistent at all times.

XII   Thou shalt NOT force nor use force on your dog.

XIII   Thou shalt walk away when frustrated with your dog.

XIV   Thou shalt NOT use aversive therapy or gadgets.

XV   Thou shalt enjoy your dog and have fun!

Author's Note

My hope is, having read and maybe re-read this book, you'll have more understanding and patience when your dog does what it does, and be able to help it modify its behaviour to suit you.

And in order for your dog to modify its behaviour, you will have to modify yours.

Don't give up when the going gets tough, because it will. Behaviour will change in all areas, sometimes initially not in the direction you'd like. When you seek to change a situation, things may get worse before they better. Embrace it – it means you are getting your dog to think.

Take heart that you have made changes, you have got your dog to think about you and its relationship with you. The dog will have to adapt; it's always got what it wanted, when it wanted, but now the tables have turned and it's got to ask questions. What's changed? You have! Keep it up, and the dog will come round if you are consistent and keep going.

Dogs are not naughty, they are just dogs; they have no hidden agenda to take over or bug you. And they have to work it out for themselves. Welcome the fact that your dog does the wrong thing as you will have the knowledge now to put it right.

I've said it many times throughout this book – whenever you put a dog right, do it with no speech, no eye contact and no emotion. Your dog will then be able to interpret your total message, rather than try to understand only your words.

If you treat your dog's issues as a challenge, not a problem, you will succeed.

Why does your dog do that?

Because it's a dog, of course. And your dog can only ever be a dog.

The PURE Dog Listening Seminars

If you'd like to learn more, please visit the website – www.puredog-listeners.com – and join me on one of my seminars. You can also visit my Facebook page, PURE Dog Listeners, or follow me on Twitter @ puredoglisteners.

Index